Starting a MINI-BUSINESS

A Guidebook for Seniors

Revised Edition

by Nancy Olsen

Illustrated by Sara Boore

Fair Oaks Publishing Co.
Sunnyvale, California

Graphics by Susan Cronin-Paris

Printed in the United States of America

Published by Fair Oaks Publishing Company
941 Populus Place, Sunnyvale, CA 94086
(408) 732-1078

Library of Congress Cataloging-in-Publication Data

Olsen, Nancy, 1939 -
    Starting a mini-business.

    Bibliography: p.
    Includes index.

    1. Home-based businesses--United States. 2. New
business enterprises--United States. I. Title.
HD62.7.046 1988   658.1'141   88-81194
ISBN 0-933271-02-6 (pbk.)

Table of Contents

Foreward

Mary K. Kouri, Ph.D.

You're part of a new breed of seniors. Vigorous, healthy, and curious, you're not at all ready for a retirement life of full-time rest and leisure. What you're after is re-engagement, with a new mix of interests and commitments. Perhaps you're even thinking about starting a very small business of your own.

Many men and women at this stage of life want to balance service to others, personal growth, and some form of work. You've worked all your life, to be sure, but now seek an occupational activity that reflects your convictions and conforms to your pace. And possibly you'd like the extras that a straight retirement income won't always allow. A mini-business may be just what you're looking for.

What *do* you want at this time in your life? As you consider this question, give your dreams and desires equal billing with the "I shoulds" and "I musts." This will free you to look at all the options. With many of your heavy financial obligations and career pressures behind you, you can indulge your curiosity and move in directions that were perhaps impractical ten or twenty years ago. You can choose work that is interesting, fun, and challenging.

Have you used skills in your hobbies that you would love to turn into a regular occupation? Is there a service just begging to be done in your neighborhood or community? Have you always had a yen to run a business with certain standards of quality? Working for yourself can help you satisfy these dreams.

The changing population also encourages the development of new businesses. For example, the growing numbers of single working parents and frail elderly need special products and services that mammoth corporations and agencies cannot supply. Your maturity, integrity, flexible schedule, and experience are a perfect match for many of these and other emerging needs.

Nancy Olsen has included some valuable exercises in the opening chapters of *Starting a Mini-Business* that will help you decide whether to establish your own business and what it should be. Her approach is humane and intelligent, keeping in sight the legitimate expectation for profit as well as satisfaction from your labors.

I've recommended *Starting a Mini-Business* to hundreds of men and women in life planning and retirement workshops, articles, and counseling. You will do yourself a service by reading it. Use its guidance to further your growth and prosperity, and to enrich the community which needs and sustains you. Relish the fruits of your work in good health, peace, and joy.

Mary K. Kouri, Ph.D., is a career counselor and gerontologist with Human Growth and Development Associates in Denver, Colorado. She is the author of numerous articles and *Elderlife: A Time to Give--A Time to Receive.* Her next book, *Wonder and Insight*, will be published in 1989.

Chapter 1
Starting Out

When Bob retired from the insurance business at the age of 59, he was surprised to find himself bored and restless. He enjoyed playing golf, but the Minnesota weather wasn't always cooperative. Besides, as much as he loved the game, he needed something more to engage his interest and keep him active. "I was going crazy," he recalls with a laugh, "and driving my wife crazy too."

The problem was solved when Bob learned that an old friend, also retired, was unable to keep up with his business of repairing, refinishing and custom-building golf clubs. Bob jumped at the chance to learn this unique set of skills and take on jobs that his overworked friend was being forced to turn down. After working alongside this craftsman for six weeks and investing $1800 in equipment and supplies, Bob was ready to take on jobs of his own.

Word of Bob's service spread rapidly to golf clubs and sporting goods shops, and soon he had as much work as he wanted, enough to keep him busy two or three hours a day for nine months of the year. With this schedule, he still has plenty of time for his own golf game, and can continue spending his winters in Arizona.

Bob's business brings in several thousand extra dollars a year, but it's not the additional income that gives him a boost so much as the fun he is having and the sense of accomplishment he feels. "It's an ego trip," he confesses. "It's great being an expert in something special and making other golfers so happy. They're ecstatic when their clubs are just right for them."

Out in California, Helen was facing a different sort of problem. Her husband had just retired and with one child still in college, Helen was a little concerned about making ends meet. Perhaps, she thought, it was time to do something about an idea that had been in the back of her mind for years--start a gardening business. She loved flowers and was always being complimented on the bright beds of annuals that surrounded her suburban home. Why not put her skills to work?

A homemaker all her married life, Helen was initially hesitant about plunging into the world of business. So she sought her first customers among her own neighbors. As her confidence increased, she approached some firms in an industrial park nearby, and now plants and maintains the flower beds for a number of these companies. An adult daughter works with her as a partner, allowing Helen to take on jobs that require more strength than she alone possesses, as well as giving her the time flexibility needed to care for a bed-ridden relative and to travel a bit with her husband. Helen is very pleased with the way things have worked out; she thinks her life has just the right balance of free time and active involvement.

Jane was in her mid-50's when she returned to Arizona from service in the Peace Corps. While considering where next to put her energies, she stayed in a vacationing friend's home, tending the animals and plants, and keeping a general watch on things. One day, she looked around her and had an idea. Surely other vacationing homeowners needed the security of knowing that someone was keeping an eye on their property and caring for their pets. This was the beginning of Housesitting Security Services, a business that places responsible retirees in homes while the owners are away. Jane is thrilled with her brainchild. Not only is she earning a good income herself, she is also providing employment to other seniors and meeting a community need.

Stanley, a Colorado resident, took up lapidary as a retirement hobby, but didn't know what to do with all the polished stones that resulted from this interest. A jewelry course provided the answer. Stanley now combines silver and stones into necklaces, bracelets, brooches and belt buckles, and finds a ready market for his beautiful creations at craft fairs and boutiques. To further supplement his income and to share his skills and enthusiasm, Stanley also offers classes in the very subjects that were new to him not long before. Stanley is delighted with all he has learned since he retired and with the new activities and involvements that have become part of his life. The extra money comes in handy too.

Bob, Helen, Jane and Stanley are real people. Their stories are typical of a growing phenomenon across the United States. In Oklahoma, 69-year old Marge earns $5,000 a year selling her famous pound cake, chiefly by mail order. A group of older women in Washington, D.C., have organized a professional baby-sitting service. A retired Minnesota couple operates a picture framing business, keeping costs low by using old frames they find at flea markets and refinish themselves. An early-rising Connecticut retiree has begun a telephone wake-up service. From computer research in Oregon to worm-farming in Florida, seniors are starting their own small-scale, home-based businesses.

Activities of this nature are appropriately called "mini-businesses," since even the term "small-business" suggests an undertaking that is more demanding and grander in scale than these part-time endeavors. What has caused the surge of interest in mini-businesses? Why are so many seniors with no previous business experience choosing to work in this way?

Inflation is, of course, one answer. Retirement incomes, whether from social security, pensions or investments, are often insufficient to allow today's retirees to enjoy the life of leisure they had expected. But continuing to work full-time is seldom ideal either. Most seniors seek supplemental, rather than full-time, incomes. They want a part-time activity that doesn't infringe too much on the free time and flexibility they had been anticipating for their retirement years. Many find that a mini-business fills this need.

But money is not the only reason seniors are attracted to mini-businesses. Having a productive, useful and challenging life activity is another. Although many workers look forward to the day when they can leave the 9 to 5 world behind, they often discover that a life of unalloyed leisure is about as desirable as a diet composed entirely of dessert. "You can't fish seven days a week," says one retiree. "I need to be with people, exercise whatever brain I have, and get some excitement out of life," says another.

The average person who retires at age 65 can expect to live another fifteen to twenty years, and thanks to advances in the field of health care, most of those years will be vigorous, active ones. To fully enjoy this lengthy retirement period means, for many, having some sort of on-going work activity. Some choose volunteer work, others part-time employment. But for those who have always dreamed of being their own boss, a mini-business is often the answer. Mini-businesses provide the things that seniors seek in their work lives--a self-determined work schedule, the stimulation of learning new skills, and opportunities to be useful to others. And there is nothing like operating a successful business, even a very small one, to bring a sense of accomplishment and personal satisfaction.

Questions and Concerns

Although many seniors are intrigued by the idea of starting their own mini-businesses, they sometimes also have fears and doubts. Here are some of the most common:

"I've heard that half of all businesses fail within two years. The odds would be against me." The statistics on business failure vary somewhat, depending on the source consulted, but it cannot be denied that they are frighteningly high. They are also somewhat misleading. The term "failure" is a powerful one, suggesting financial and psychological catastrophe. "Termination" is a more neutral word, and more accurate too, since many so-called "failures" are far from catastrophic. Businesses may be terminated after several years of operation for a variety of reasons. For example, the business might be surviving nicely but is not as lucrative as the owner(s) had hoped. Or the interests of the individuals involved have changed, causing them to move on to another line of work. They may even have chosen to retire from work altogether.

Even when an owner unwillingly closes down a business, financial disaster may not be implied. If the amount of money invested was small, little has been lost. Whether such an event is psychologically troubling will depend upon the attitude of the person involved. Some *feel* like "failures" and give up; others bounce back, build on what they have learned, and try again. The owners of mini-businesses, in particular, oftentimes terminate their activities with no financial loss and little regret.

In addition to all of this, it is important to know that your chances of success can be greatly increased by careful planning. The information in this book can help you "beat the odds."

"I need a regular income; I can't handle the uncertainty of not knowing how much I'll make each month." If you feel this way, then running a business is probably not for you. Business income does vary, and paid employment is more apt to provide the security of a regular paycheck. But some mini-businesspeople look at things this way: "If I worked for someone else, I could always be laid off or have my job cut back. My boss might decide I'm too old or not fast enough. Despite the irregular income, I feel more in charge of my own financial future by being on my own."

"I'm receiving social security benefits and don't want to lose this source of income." It is true that social security payments are reduced for individuals whose earnings exceed a certain level. This level changes from year to year. In 1988 it is $6,120 for people under the age of 65 and $8,400 for those age 65 to 69. (There is no limit for those 70 and over.) If you earn more than the allowed amount, your social security benefits are reduced by $1 for every $2 in excess earnings.

In evaluating this information, it is important to realize that what counts as business earnings is your "net profit," the amount left after all of your business expenses have been paid (see Chapters 7 and 8 for more information on how net profit is calculated). Most mini-businesses, especially during the early years, end up with net profits which fall considerably below the social security limitation. Some retired mini-businesspeople do this deliberately; if it seems that they might otherwise earn too much, they cut back a bit on their efforts.

Even if you do earn more than the allowed amount, remember that it is only the excess that is penalized, and that the penalty is only 50%. If your mini-business does this well, you will still be money ahead, and will also have the thrill of seeing your business succeed.

More details about the "earnings test" are available from your local social security office. Several helpful pamphlets on this subject can be had for the asking, and the staff will be happy to answer your questions.

"I don't think I have what it takes to run a business." Maybe yes, maybe no. Starting a mini-business will not be the right step for everyone. To make a go of business, even the smallest of mini-businesses, requires being well-organized, persistent, self-motivated, trustworthy, and people-oriented. How do you measure up on these traits? **Exercise 1**, adapted from the pamphlet "Going into Business," published by the U.S. Small Business Administration, is a way for you to rate yourself. (You will find all of the exercises together in the appendix at the back of this book.)

When you have completed Exercise 1, look at the pattern of your responses. If most of your checks are beside the first answer, you probably have the qualities needed to operate a mini-business. If most of your checks are beside the second answer, you may find it difficult to start and manage a business on your own, but might do fine with one or more partners or co-workers who are strong in the areas where you are lacking. If most of your checks are beside the third answer, the business world is probably not the place for you.

Of course, a little quiz such as this provides only a sampling of qualities, and the results should be given careful thought but not taken too literally. The purpose of the exercise is to provoke self-analysis. Most seniors have what it takes to establish and run a successful mini-business, but some will decide that a mini-business is not right for them. It is perfectly all right to conclude that your strengths are in other areas and that other retirement activities will bring you greater satisfaction. But if you think you'll enjoy the challenge that a mini-business offers and want to learn more, this book can be your guide.

"But I don't know anything about advertising, bookkeeping and all the other things involved in running a business." Perhaps not, but you can learn! Besides, in most mini-businesses, these tasks can be handled quite simply and creatively. And that is what this book is about.

Why This Book Was Written

The shelves of bookstores and libraries are weighted down with books on starting and managing small businesses. But the book you have in your hands is very different. It comes from my experience at New Ways to Work, a non-profit job counseling center in Palo Alto, California, where for a number of years I worked with seniors who wanted to learn about starting mini-businesses. From beginners who had no idea about the type of business they might undertake to those who were already tentatively underway, the need for practical knowledge was great. Yet there was little in the way of written materials we could recommend. Most of the existing "small business" literature seemed to assume that its readers would be taking out sizeable loans, developing complex marketing strategies, and aiming to grow ever bigger. Such books were more intimidating than helpful. Down-to-earth information suitable for the older person wanting a small-scale, part-time business activity was hard to find. So we developed our own, more appropriate materials which I now want to share with a wider audience. Hence this book, and here's what makes it unique:

• It is written specifically for those over 55, retired or preparing for retirement. Older people often have special health, income and social circumstances that this book takes into account. (On the other hand, the principles of starting a mini-business are pretty much the same for all age groups. Artists and craftspeople who want to develop their talents into a business while continuing to hold down a regular job, young mothers seeking a part-time work activity compatible with their family responsibilities, and energetic teenagers eager for extra spending money are among those who will also find the information in this book of value.)

• It discusses only low-cost, low-risk, part-time businesses that can easily be tackled by men and women with no previous experience. It presents practical information in a straightforward way, using everyday vocabulary rather than confusing business terminology. While not glossing over hard realities (such as taxes!), it avoids introducing complexities that mini-businesses are unlikely to encounter.

• The book has a value bias, emphasizing personal satisfaction and community service more than the accumulation of profits. This does not mean I advocate an unbusinesslike approach or think it is wrong to make money in a mini-business. On the contrary, this book will show you how to be well-organized and keep good records as a step toward reaching your financial goals. But my experience tells me that everyone needs satisfaction from work and a feeling of contributing to the well-being of others. To my way of thinking, achieving these ends is just as important a measure of success as the size of one's bank account.

• The "rugged individualist" is not the hero or heroine of this book. Rather, I stress the value of working together with others. This is partly because of my own commitment to help build a cooperative society. But even more, I know how important it is that the retired avoid the dangers of social isolation. A mini-business can either be a powerful tool for staying in touch with others or an excuse for "going it alone." I believe it is healthier, and more fun, to let your mini-business be a vehicle for social involvement.

• Written exercises provide a way to apply the book's information to the planning of your own mini-business. These can be photocopied if you don't want to write in the book itself or if you need extra copies. (As an alternative, most of the exercises lend themselves to being discussed out loud with a partner taking notes.) If you complete the exercises as you go along, you will be well on your way to starting a successful mini-business by the time you finish Chapter 11.

My aim has been to write a truly useful book, one that will supply you with the knowledge you need to establish a satisfying mini-business. Small-scale businesses have brought a sense of purpose, good times and extra dollars into the lives of many seniors. I hope you will join them.

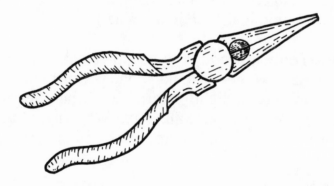

For More Information

"Is unretirement in your future?" by Alice M. Pytak. DYNAMIC YEARS, July-August 1984, pp. 24-28.
> *An upbeat article that stresses the benefits of continuing involvement in the world of work. Self-employment is one of several options discussed.*

HOW TO START A PROFITABLE RETIREMENT BUSINESS, by Arthur Lieber. Pilot Books, Babylon, NY, 1985.
> *This small booklet provides a good overview of business ideas and issues of concern to seniors.*

GOING INTO BUSINESS FOR YOURSELF: NEW BEGINNINGS AFTER 50, by Ina Lee Selden. AARP Books, Scott-Foresman & Co., DesPlaines, IL, 1988.
This new book includes a wealth of information on such topics as business plans and raising capital. An important resource for the senior who aims to start a business that is larger than mini-sized.

"Can You Get Rich in Retirement?" by S.R. Kleinhen. DYNAMIC YEARS, July-August 1980, pp. 41-43.
Considerations involved in starting a mini-business, useful even for those whose ambitions do not include "getting rich."

"Home Work for Seniors," by Raymond Schuessler. COURIER, April 1982, p. 51.
A short article packed with ideas for mini-businesses suitable for retirees.

Chapter 2
Getting Ideas

After years of working for someone else, many retirees are enthusiastic about the possibility of being in business for themselves. But they wonder what kind of business to start?

Perhaps you already know the answer to this question. Your life-long hobby has been photography, and you now want nothing more than to earn a little money from this treasured avocation. Or you have seen the need in your community for a support service for families of cancer patients and have already met with several friends to discuss joining together to offer such a service. If this is your situation, you may wish to skip to the section entitled "Defining Your Business Idea" at the end of this chapter. On the other hand, most people find it fun to explore new ideas. And in this process, you may discover a mini-business that will suit you even better than the one you now have in mind.

Brainstorming New Business Ideas

The most satisfying and successful mini-businesses are based, not on someone else's idea of a "sure-fire money-maker," but on the things *you* value. What are the activities you most enjoy? What are your special skills and talents? What community groups, problems or political causes are of special concern to you? The method of brainstorming is a good way to come up with ideas for mini-businesses that respond to interests such as these.

Brainstorming is a technique for releasing the natural creativity that is present in individuals of all ages. Too often people pre-censor their thoughts, telling themselves, "it won't work," "people will laugh," "I'm too old (or young)," and so on. Brainstorming is a way of avoiding this stifling tendency. It simply means coming up with as many ideas on a subject as possible, no matter how far-fetched they may seem, and withholding judgment until after the list is finished. Inventive new solutions and approaches frequently emerge in this process.

Brainstorming works best in a group where each person's contributions stimulate new thoughts in the others. So, if possible, complete Exercises 2-5 together with several of your friends who are also thinking of starting mini-businesses or who would enjoy helping you get yours off the ground.

Here's how it works: Each potential businessperson completes the first column of each exercise by him/herself. Then the group brainstorms ideas for mini-businesses based on the items listed in that column. No comments are allowed until the list is as long as the group can make it. You can imagine how many ideas will be generated in this way. For example, if you list only five items for each of the four exercises, and if the group can think of only five ideas for each item, you will end up with a total of 100 mini-business ideas! Probably your list will be much longer. Of course, many of these ideas will be impractical, uninteresting to you, or just plain silly. That doesn't matter, because some good ones will have emerged too.

Begin with **Exercise 2**, in the appendix, which asks you to focus on the things you most enjoy. This might include hobbies, daily activities, or special occasions. When Frank did this exercise, he listed the following pleasures: walking the dog, square-dancing, watching baseball games on television, baking bread, a week at the beach every summer, attending birthday parties for the grandchildren, and writing letters to the editor of the newspaper.

To show how brainstorming works, here is a partial list of the mini-businesses his group thought of in response to Frank's interest in walking the dog: operate a morning and evening dog-walking service, manufacture dog collars or leashes, make identification tags for pets, give obedience lessons to dogs, care for pets while their owners are away on vacation, make raincoats for dogs, manufacture an improved "pooper scooper," take and sell photographs of scenery viewed while walking the dog, take photos of dogs in the out-of-doors and make them into notecards, make Walkman cassette tapes called "Music to Walk the Dog By."

The group was equally creative in coming up with mini-businesses based on the other things Frank enjoys. With this exercise alone, Frank had over 90 ideas to consider. You will probably do just as well. Even if you must do the exercise without the aid of a group, you will get lots of ideas if you let your thoughts roam freely.

Exercise 3, calling for you to list your special skills and talents, may result in some overlap with Exercise 2. After all, people often gain pleasure from the things they do well. But it should also generate some new items. In Frank's case, baking bread, square dancing, and writing letters appeared on both lists (Frank thought of himself as being pretty good at all three), but Exercise 3 also resulted in: repairing small appliances, keeping track of household expenses, keeping a conversation going, finding things for the grandchildren to do on rainy days, organizing people to get things done (he had started the square dance club as well as several other community activities), knowledge of current events, and population research (this was his pre-retirement occupation; although he wasn't keen on continuing this line of work, he avoided censoring his thoughts). How many mini-businesses can you think of that rely on Frank's skill in keeping a conversation going? on his knowledge of current events?

Exercise 4 provides an opportunity to consider ways of developing a mini-business based squarely on an effort to improve the world. What community groups do you care about most? What are the problems faced by your community or our nation that concern you? What political causes do you support? Frank had a lot of fun with this exercise. Here is his list: PEACE, housing shortage, cost of health care, lack of meaningful summer activities for young teenagers (too old for camp, too young to get jobs), natural nutrition, Gray Panthers, church men's group, Red Cross blood drive.

Despite his initial doubts that any of these interests and concerns could result in a mini-business, Frank was pleased at the results of brainstorming. Among the better ideas, Frank thought, were manufacturing bumper stickers with peace-related slogans, starting a service to place young teens in responsible volunteer positions, and writing a natural foods cookbook.

Would you like more ideas? Then complete **Exercise 5**. Choose from the three options given, or use blank paper and do all three. Among the *objects or spaces* available to you might be: typewriter, camera, sewing machine, pruning shears, lawn mower, home computer, rowboat, automobile, spare room, garage, attic, back yard, tree house. Let your imagination go. Your list of *jobs other people do from time to time* might include: washing windows, giving parties, doing income taxes, shampooing carpets, sharpening knives and scissors, tuning pianos, trimming trees, selecting Christmas presents, planting annuals.

Finally, a mini-business need not rely on already existing interests and talents; perhaps you'll want to use Exercise 5 to list things you'd *like to learn to do* in your retirement--write poetry, master the use of a personal computer, repair your own car, do yoga. If you must first develop a skill before turning it into a mini-business, it will naturally take more time to get your venture underway, and this may make some mini-business possibilities less feasible than others. But that is no reason to avoid considering such ideas. The rewards from mastering a new area of expertise are great and may well be worth the additional effort required.

What about books that provide lists of business ideas? Although brainstorming is usually the best way of coming up with a mini-business suited to your own individual interests, sometimes "idea books" are also helpful in stimulating the imagination. A few of the more useful ones are listed at the end of this chapter.

Defining Your Business Idea

If you have completed Exercises 2-5, and/or consulted one or more of the books listed below, you will have a long list of possible mini-businesses. Of course, many of these can be ruled out right away as obviously impractical or of no interest to you. But there will certainly be some that appeal to you as useful, stimulating and do-able activities that may also have the potential to bring in the extra dollars you seek.

Now is the time to select one of these mini-business ideas for further evaluation. To begin, simply pick the one that intuitively feels "best." If upon closer study you discover that it has some problems, you can always return to your list and make another choice.

How, then, can you judge whether your chosen idea is a "good" one? The next chapter will examine this important question from several points of view. But first it is necessary to be able to describe your potential mini-business in a clear way. You won't be able to judge the merit of your idea until you are sure just what it is. Suppose you are the photography enthusiast mentioned at the beginning of this chapter. Will your mini-business involve studio portraits (of families? graduating high school students? company presidents? pets?) or will you take art shots of beautiful scenery which you frame and sell at fairs?

These are two quite different businesses, requiring different equipment and skills, having different customers, and fitting into your life in different ways. And these are only two of the many possible options for a photography business! Is photography a good idea for a mini-business? The answer may depend on just what type of photography you have in mind.

Exercise 6 will help you clarify your chosen mini-business idea. As you work on this exercise, you will experience the excitement of seeing a hazy image come into focus as the beginnings of a concrete plan. You will be on your way!

For More Information

A wealth of ideas for mini-businesses may be found in the following:

555 WAYS TO EARN EXTRA MONEY, by Jay Conrad Levinson. Holt, Rinehart and Winston, New York, NY, 1982.

EARN MONEY AT HOME: OVER 100 IDEAS FOR BUSINESSES REQUIRING LITTLE OR NO CAPITAL, by Peter Davidson. McGraw Hill, New York, NY, 1981.

HOMEBASED BUSINESSES, by Beverly Neuer Feldman. Till Press, Los Angeles, CA, 1983.

THE #1 HOME BUSINESS BOOK, by George and Sandra Delany. Liberty House, TAB Books, Inc., Blue Ridge Summit, PA, 1981.

Chapter 3
Deciding to Go Ahead

Y ou now have an idea for your mini-business, and perhaps you have no doubt that it's just what you want to do. It's an activity you've always loved, you already have all the necessary equipment and materials, and you know that your product or service is one that's badly needed in your community. If so, you may want to skip this chapter and turn directly to the information on "Establishing Your Home Business." But if you are less sure, if you want to evaluate your business idea more systematically before deciding to go ahead with it, this chapter is for you.

Is your business idea a good one? Certainly, if you can answer "yes" to the following questions: *Will it satisfy my personal needs and goals? Can I afford the starting costs? Will other people be interested in what I want to provide? Will it meet my income needs?*

Personal Satisfaction

Perhaps you have chosen to start a mini-business because you need the extra money to pay your living expenses. Does this mean that personal satisfaction is a luxury that pertains only to those who already have adequate retirement incomes? Definitely not! If earning a good salary is your primary goal, you will have to be more careful in selecting the type of business to pursue and in your plans for carrying it out, but you need not ignore your other desires and goals in making a choice. On the contrary, a business is more likely to be financially successful if you enjoy what you do. This is because your motivation will be much greater if you love your work and believe in its importance.

In Chapter 2, you had the opportunity to generate business ideas based on your interests, skills and values. These were derived primarily from the *content* of the work--golf photos for the golfing (or photography) buff, peace-related bumper stickers for the individual devoted to world peace. Finding a mini-business idea that relates to your own concerns and enthusiasms is one key to personal satisfaction.

But the *style* of working is also important. Just as people have different interests and skills, they also prefer different types of working environments and have different goals they hope to accomplish through their work. Do you crave new experiences? leadership? tranquility? physical activity? Is it among your goals to serve a particular group of people or to offer a durable product in our throw-away era?

Exercise 7 lists a variety of needs and goals that seniors have expressed in talking about their work lives. It is only a partial list, to provide examples, and you will probably want to add to it. This exercise will help you identify the items that are of importance to you. Once you have done this, you can examine your proposed mini-business to see whether it is likely to bring you personal satisfaction.

Of course, one activity cannot satisfy every need, so you should not expect that the match between the two columns of Exercise 7 will be a perfect one. But it is important to ascertain whether your business idea is compatible with the things you care about. For example, many retirees place a high value on flexible working hours. They want to feel free to enjoy drop-in visitors, take time off for recreational pursuits, or simply relax a bit now and then. Large numbers of mini-businesses allow this kind of time flexibility. Others don't.

Infant care is an example of a mini-business that demands fixed daily hours. Working parents count on regular care being available and cannot be expected to make last-minute alternative arrangements except in the most extreme emergency. The senior who hopes to start a mini-business involving babies, but who also wishes to have time flexibility, will need to consider a business other than infant care for working parents. Can you think of a mini-business that will bring personal satisfaction on both of these dimensions?

Starting Costs

In most cases, seniors starting mini-businesses should aim for spending as little money as possible. Younger people who are establishing full-time businesses that they hope will eventually support themselves and their families may need to spend tens of thousands of dollars for a facility, equipment and merchandise. However, should they be so unlucky as to lose a portion of their investment, they still have many working years to repay loans and rebuild their savings. The circumstances of seniors are different, and few are willing to risk their financial security to get a mini-business going.

What are the characteristics of a low-cost (and therefore low-risk) business? Generally speaking, service businesses cost less to start than product businesses. But a product business that grows out of an established hobby need not be expensive, since you will probably already have all of the necessary equipment and materials. For example, the woodworking enthusiast who plans to construct doll houses will probably already own the saws, sanders and other power tools needed to get this mini-business underway. If, on the other hand, your business requires new equipment or an extensive inventory or a great deal of advertising, it will cost more to establish.

Of course, "low-cost" means different things to different people. Some seniors would feel quite a pinch if they had to spend $100, while others could safely invest several thousand. **Exercise 8** will enable you to estimate your probable starting costs, but only you can decide how much is "too much."

Should seniors ever consider borrowing money to start a mini-business? Only rarely is this advisable, particularly for those with no previous business experience. Bank loans are never appropriate in such circumstances, but you might consider a small loan from family or friends. If so, treat the transaction in a businesslike fashion. Put your agreement in writing so you will have no unpleasant misunderstandings. When will you pay the money back? At what rate of interest?

Another alternative is to ask one or more family members or friends to pre-pay for your product or service. For example, suppose you lack the money to purchase a caulking gun and the other equipment needed to start a home weatherization service. You know this service will be in great demand in your community. Some of your friends might be willing to pay in advance for their weatherization so as to provide you with the necessary cash. Again, it is a good idea to formalize such an arrangement with a written agreement.

Customer Interest

The customers or potential customers (or clients) of a business are known as its "market," and learning about their tastes, buying habits, values, and patterns of living is called "market research." Many business owners never do research of this kind, and trust their own intuition in deciding such matters as what to offer, how much to charge, and where to advertise. Or, if the business is a low-cost one, they may follow the method of trial-and-error. They try out a particular product or service, advertise it in a particular way, and see what kind of response they get. If something doesn't seem to be working, it is altered or abandoned.

Both of these approaches are perfectly legitimate. However, some mini-businesspeople prefer to begin with a clearer idea of whether there is an interest in what they plan to offer. "Market research" sounds like a formidable undertaking, but in reality can be very simple and straightforward. Here are some possible ways to go about it.

Existing Businesses. Businesses which provide similar products or services are ordinarily referred to as the "competition," but all too often the use of this term seems to encourage an inappropriately ruthless attitude. No one should set up a mini-business aiming to take away another's livelihood. What you will usually find is that your business is somewhat different and thus appeals to a different "market." Or you will be located in a different part of town.

As a result of these considerations, it is generally more realistic to think of businesspeople who do similar kinds of work as colleagues and not competitors. By sharing information and resources, cooperatively oriented businesspeople frequently find they can contribute to one another's success rather than detract from it.

Nell, who had retired to a lakeside resort community, wished to open a used book exchange from her glassed-in front porch. (This type of home business may not be permissible in your locality; see Chapter 4.) She planned to concentrate on novels and other light reading for summer visitors.

Before beginning, Nell contacted the one bookstore in town. This shop, as it happened, did not carry used books, and the owner revealed that many vacationers seemed unwilling to pay new book prices for casual reading material. Nell realized that her mini-business would fill a need, and that it would complement the offerings of the already existing shop. The two proprietors could refer customers to each other and both benefit.

Therefore, do not hesitate to talk to others about your plans. Ask them about their customers. Do they have plenty of business? Are there services or products that customers seem to want that the existing business is not able or does not wish to supply? What groups of people does the business attract, and which groups do not or cannot take advantage of its services? Answers to questions such as these will help you to determine whether there is a niche for your own mini-business, or perhaps give you some ideas about possible ways of modifying what you plan to offer.

Potential Customers. The people (or businesses) that you hope will purchase your product or use your service can also provide valuable information and advice. Over the years, Adela had received numerous compliments on the baby sweaters she knitted for family members and friends. She hoped to start a mini-business by selling her sweaters at the Senior Center Craft Shop. Before knitting a number of sweaters to bring in, she talked with the manager of the shop. How many baby sweaters were already being carried there? How well did the sweaters sell? What colors and styles did the customers prefer? Were there any other knitted items that were popular with the customers?

From this conversation Adela concluded that she would probably be able to sell quite a few of her sweaters in this way, but that she might also want to expand her mini-business to include booties and other less costly items, since the demand for these was even greater than for sweaters. She also learned which colors and patterns were customer favorites, so she could make items that would sell better.

Bud hoped to start another type of mini-business--toy repair. He thought this would be a good way to bring together his fondness for children, the pleasure he felt in working with his hands, and his concern about resource conservation. But would there be a market for his service? He feared that today's parents might be more inclined to throw broken toys away than to have them repaired.

Bud found the answer to his question by talking informally with many of the young parents in his neighborhood and at his church. He learned that parents were interested in having only certain types of toys repaired. One of these was dolls. After some thought Bud decided to go ahead with his mini-business, but to specialize in doll repair. He called himself the Doll Doctor, and eventually offered his skilled services to adult doll collectors as well as broken-hearted children. This business was a bit different from the one he had originally planned, but was just as satisfying.

Talking to potential customers is the most common way of learning about their interest in your product or service, but it is also possible to observe their behavior. For example, Adela could have browsed in the Craft Shop for an hour or two all the while noticing the types of items that customers seemed to find especially attractive. Bud might have strolled around his neighborhood on trash collection day, observing the number and type of broken toys that were being discarded.

Other Resources. Where else might you find information and advice about the feasibility of your planned mini-business? The answer to this question will be different for different types of businesses. One possibility is *suppliers*, the people from whom you will purchase the materials or products needed for your business. They are in touch with others who are already conducting businesses similar to the one you want to start. From this experience they will be able to tell you a great deal about the problems and successes others might be having, the items that sell best, and so on.

Trade and professional associations may also be useful. There is an association to represent almost every type of business imaginable. These groups maintain membership lists, compile statistics on such topics as purchasing patterns, and have information on standard rates and prices. The person at the reference desk of your local library can help you find out which association is most appropriate to your mini-business.

The *U.S. Census of Population* can supply an amazing range of facts about your community, some of which may be helpful in your market research. From census reports you can learn how many families in your community are large or small, have pre-schoolers or teenagers, own their homes or rent, have incomes of a certain size, work in particular industries, own various appliances, and much more. Suppose you were planning to start morning yoga classes for retired people between the ages of 55 and 75. Census data could inform you of the number of such individuals living in your town.

Other potentially helpful sources of information, particularly concerning local business trends, are your *chamber of commerce*, *shopping center managers*, and your local *newspaper*. Can you think of other places to turn for assistance in learning about your market?

Conclusion. There is no magic formula to tell you with certainty whether the market for your mini-business will be large enough. But collecting information from existing businesses, potential customers, and other sources can help you improve your guesswork. Will customers be interested in what you plan to offer? **Exercise 9** provides a way for you to summarize your thinking on this matter.

The result of market research is sometimes discouraging. You may even decide to give up on your idea and turn to an entirely different type of business. Much more often, as was true for both Adela and Bud, you will learn of ways to change your idea a bit to make it work better.

Of course, these are also things you can discover as you go along. If your starting costs are not great, and if you are enjoying yourself, it doesn't hurt to learn from experience. An inquisitive spirit and a mind open to change will allow you to make adjustments as needed.

Income Needs

Some seniors are interested in operating mini-businesses for reasons that have little to do with making money, while others count on the extra dollars that a mini-business can provide. If you are among those with specific monetary goals, you must necessarily pay close attention to the income-generating potential of your mini-business idea.

Of course, it is never possible to know with certainty how much you will actually earn from a particular type of business. But there are ways to estimate how much business activity is required to result in a particular level of income. Whether you are able to achieve your financial target will then depend on a variety of factors, including: how much time you are able or willing to invest, how thoughtfully you have carried out and evaluated the results of your market research, and how creative you can be in finding customers.

To examine the relationship between amount of business activity and probable income necessitates reading further along in this book. The information in Chapter 5, although designed to help you establish a price for your product or service, will also be of value in estimating the amount of money you may be able to earn from your mini-business endeavor.

For More Information

WHAT COLOR IS YOUR PARACHUTE? by Richard Bolles. Ten-Speed Press, Berkeley, CA, revised every year.
> *Personal satisfaction from work is the theme of this book. It provides a wide variety of exercises to help identify skills, values and preferred working environments. A best-seller, and with good reason.*

HONEST BUSINESS: A SUPERIOR STRATEGY FOR STARTING AND MANAGING YOUR OWN BUSINESS, by Michael Phillips and Salli Rasberry. Random House, New York, NY, 1981.
> *This book argues for the benefits of spending as little money as possible when starting up, and for proceeding slowly and cautiously. In addition, it includes a wealth of sound, if sometimes unconventional, advice on all aspects of running a small business.*

"Research Your Market" (MA4.019)
A low-cost pamphlet available from the Small Business Administration. For a complete list and ordering information, call your local office of the S.B.A. (look under U.S. Government in the telephone book) or write to P.O. Box 15434, Fort Worth, TX, 76119. Ask for SBA-115A.

Chapter 4
Establishing Your Home Business

It's time to get underway. You have an idea that excites you and that you think will work. What are the steps involved in putting your idea into action? That is what the rest of this book is all about. In this chapter you will learn how to take the first steps, those involved in setting yourself up as a home-based businessperson.

Choosing a Name

It is not necessary to have a special business name. You can just as easily be Magdalena Sanchez, Gardener, as "Green Thumb Gardeners" or Hansen-Jorgenson Graphics as "The Olde-Tyme Graphics Company." And it costs money to register a business name.

Nonetheless, many people enjoy having a business name, or they find that this helps them to take their work more seriously. Then, too, customers sometimes prefer to deal with a "company" rather than an individual.

The best business names are simple, easy to pronounce, descriptive and not too limiting. The name should tell the kind of business you do without being so specific as to prevent future shifts in direction.

For example, when George first began his mini-business, he made only leather sandals and called himself "Bay Tree Sandalworks." Later he added belts, handbags and other leather items, and his business name was no longer descriptive. At the other end of the spectrum, "The Bay Tree Company" would have given no clue at all as to the nature of the business being conducted. "Bay Tree Leatherworks" would not have been foolproof (George might have expanded into pottery or woodworking), but would have been a more appropriate original choice.

The name you choose should not be the same as any other within your county. Further, if you expect to do much business outside your own county, it is a good idea to avoid the names of businesses registered in these other places. You can find a list of registered names at the county clerk's office. Depending on how widely you plan to advertise, you may also wish to check with the department of corporations in your state to see if any large businesses have incorporated using the name you have chosen.

More information about registering business names can be found in Chapter 9.

Zoning Laws

Almost every community has laws to prevent commercial establishments from locating in residential neighborhoods. But every community also permits home businesses of some kinds. Since each town or county makes its own laws, you will need to check with your local government office (usually the planning department) if you have any questions about whether your mini-business can legally be conducted from your home.

Generally speaking, a home business is permissible if it does not create noise or generate very much additional traffic. Usually (but not always) the business may have only family members as employees. And communities are quite varied in terms of whether they allow sales from the home, and if so, how much customer traffic is permitted.

Sometimes the regulations governing home businesses are excessively strict, yet are not enforced on a regular basis. In one town, home businesses are forbidden to engage in manufacturing or to use any electrical or mechanical devices. Interpreted literally, this makes Edna a lawbreaker, since she crochets afghans for sale (a manufacturing activity), along with all of the home typists and piano teachers in town (typewriters and pianos are mechanical devices). The municipal officials are quite clear that they do not want Edna and people like her to stop what they are doing. The laws are meant to be applied only when manufacturing or the use of mechanical devices results in noise, unpleasant odors, unsightliness, or potential danger.

The lesson to be learned from this example is to avoid being overly intimidated by the letter of the law. In most communities, zoning officials check on home businesses only if there is an obvious violation or if someone complains. If you are concerned that your activities may bother your neighbors, it is a good idea to talk with them about it. You may also find it useful to consult someone who is already engaged in a home business similar to the one you plan to start.

Getting Organized

A "home-based" business is not necessarily one that is carried out at home. If you conduct bicycle tours or teach tennis, you will meet your clients in the out-of-doors. If you tune pianos, you will travel to the home of those who need your service. You may even rent a space to carry on some portion of your business activity. For example, the five women who operate The Cookie Co-op rent a church kitchen three mornings a week in order to have the space and equipment necessary to make large quantities of their "home-made" cookies and brownies. But all of these businesses are still *based* at home. This is where records are kept and telephone calls received. And every home-based business needs an office.

Your "office" may be nothing more than a desk in a corner of your bedroom or living room, or it may be much grander. By having all of your business-related materials in one place, you will be able to carry on your mini-business in an organized fashion. You may also save yourself some money on taxes (see Chapter 8). Perhaps most importantly, you will give yourself a psychological boost. You will *feel* like a businessperson.

One issue to be faced in setting up a home office is whether to install a separate business telephone. This would be advisable if you expect to receive a large number of calls and your residence telephone gets a lot of use from other members of your household. Some mini-businesses also find that it creates a more professional image to have a separate telephone. Most often, however, mini-businesses rely on their residence telephone, perhaps with an extension for the office or workshop.

An answering machine for the telephone is sometimes a worthwhile investment, particularly if you are often away. Callers are frustrated when they try to reach a business only to have the telephone ring unanswered. A taped message will let callers know when you plan to return and invite them to leave their name and number so you can get in touch with them later. The answering machine can also be turned on when you are at home, but need some uninterrupted work time.

Just as important as organizing your workspace is organizing your time. After years of living the 9 to 5 life, many retirees find it difficult to "get down to business" when they have only themselves to answer to.

It is a good idea to establish a work schedule for yourself right at the beginning. Set up a regular daily or weekly pattern. This may be based on when you feel most energetic, when you are least likely to be interrupted, when other people most need your services, or a variety of other factors. For example, Carla, who enjoys watching television but hates having "idle hands," had always worked on her weaving while viewing her favorite programs. When she decided to transform her hobby into a mini-business, she saw no reason to change this habit. She picked the three hours of each day with the best programs and used that as her work time.

Once you have established a work schedule, stick to it. Don't let trivialities, such as an unread newspaper or unwashed dishes, distract you. Solicit the cooperation of your family and friends; ask them to telephone or drop in during non-working hours. But you need not be excessively rigid either. Of course, you will take time off for special occasions and events--birthday parties, the arrival of out-of-town guests, and so on. Indeed, having this kind of flexibility is one of the nicest things about being in business for yourself.

Other Steps

A separate checking account for your mini-business is a must. If you don't have a business name, simply use your own name. But select a color and style of check that is different from your personal account to avoid getting the two accounts mixed up. Whenever you spend any money on your business (buying materials, office supplies, or whatever), use your business checkbook.

Similarly, whatever money you receive from the sales of your product or service, no matter how small, should be deposited in your business account. In this way you will have a written record of all your financial transactions--a simple but effective bookkeeping system.

Some home businesses prefer to use a post office box number as their mailing address. There are pros and cons to this strategy. You may enjoy a trip to the post office each day or find it a nuisance. A post office box number sometimes sounds more businesslike than an address which is obviously residential. But some potential customers or suppliers may fear that a post office box number signals a "fly-by-night" operation. If you decide that a post office box suits your needs, apply right away, as many stations have waiting lists.

Most mini-businesses get along without the services of a lawyer or accountant. But if you expect that your financial or legal affairs will be more complex than usual, this is a good time to make contact with these technical professionals. Ask other mini-businesspeople for recommendations. If you already have a family attorney or a tax accountant, he or she may be able to advise you about your business too. (Free or low-cost tax and legal services set up especially for seniors are usually not allowed to advise on business matters.)

If you decide that you need to engage the services of an attorney or accountant, do not hesitate to "shop around." Visit several and chat with each briefly before making up your mind which one to employ. Look for someone whose explanations are easy to understand, whose general approach is one that feels comfortable to you, and who knows about issues affecting *small* businesses. (Many business specialists are accustomed to dealing only with large corporations.) Be sure to inquire about fees.

Those operating product businesses will also want to start establishing accounts with suppliers. At the beginning you may need to pay cash for your materials or inventory, but most businesspeople try to get charge accounts set up as soon as possible. Be prepared to supply credit references and to pay your bills on time.

Consider joining business or professional associations where you can learn from and enjoy the company of others who are doing work similiar to your own. Sometimes the dues of national organizations are too steep for the mini-businessperson, but there may be an affordable local chapter. If there is no organization of mini-businesspeople in your community, why not start one? Invite your potential colleagues for a monthly potluck where you can share information and support. An occasional speaker on such topics as inexpensive advertising or tax laws regarding home businesses will add interest and bring a fresh perspective.

Do not hesitate to plunge into these activities. You may feel reluctant to telephone a city official or open a business checking account, but with each step you take, your knowledge and confidence will grow. Soon you will find yourself actually "in business," and proud of your newly acquired expertise.

For More Information

WOMEN WORKING HOME: THE HOMEBASED BUSINESS GUIDE AND DIRECTORY, Second Edition, by Marion Behr and Wendy Lazar. WWH Press, Scarsdale, NY, 1983.
A comprehensive guidebook on establishing a home business. Most of the photographs show younger women, but 95% of the advice is equally applicable to seniors and most of it to men as well as women.

HOMEMADE MONEY: THE DEFINITIVE GUIDE TO SUCCESS IN A HOME BUSINESS, Second Edition, by Barbara Brabec. Betterway Publications, White Hall, VA, 1986.
Another highly recommended "how-to" manual.

RUNNING A ONE PERSON BUSINESS, by Claude Whitmyer, Salli Rasberry, and Michael Phillips. Ten-Speed Press, Berkeley, CA, 1988.
Covers a range of topics of concern to home-based businesspeople, with a special emphasis on ways to get organized.

WORKING FROM HOME, by Paul and Sarah Edwards. Jeremy P. Tarcher, Los Angeles, CA, 1985.
> *Although oriented primarily toward "high tech" professionals, there is still much in this book that will be useful to all types of at-home buinesspeople. Covers zoning laws, time and money management, organizing a home work space, ways to avoid isolation, and other important matters.*

HOW TO GET CONTROL OF YOUR TIME AND YOUR LIFE, by Alan Lakein. New American Library Signet Books, New York, NY, 1973.
> *For those who have trouble with procrastination or disorganization, this popular book offers advice on setting priorities, making decisions, and getting things done.*

Chapter 5
Setting Prices

Deciding how much to charge for your product or service can be difficult, since it requires taking a number of facts and feelings into account, all at the same time. This is a juggling or balancing act that becomes easier with experience. The information in this chapter will help you get started.

To begin with, no mini-business should aim to lose money, so your first goal is to charge enough to cover your costs. These are of two types: (1) what you have to pay for the products you resell to your customers, called "cost of goods sold," and (2) all of the other expenses involved in operating your mini-business, called "overhead" or "operating expenses." In addition, most businesspeople hope to do more than break even; they want to be able to earn some money from their endeavors, that is, to make a profit. *Cost of goods sold*, *operating expenses* and *profit* are the three components that make up a selling price.

Components of a Selling Price

Cost of Goods Sold. Hilda sells hot dogs and soft drinks from a pushcart. The cost to her of each hot dog includes the frankfurter, the bun, the condiments (relish, sauerkraut, mustard and so on), a sheet of waxed paper to wrap it in, and several paper napkins for the customer. Of course, she buys all these in wholesale quantities and at wholesale prices, so she needs to do a little arithmetic to figure out just what it costs her to put a single hot dog in the hands of a hungry patron. The soft drinks are easier. Since she doesn't supply paper cups, her cost is simply what she paid for each can or bottle.

Hilda's business involves purchasing already-made products and reselling them. Harvey and Ted, on the other hand, are manufacturers, which means that they transform raw materials into finished products. In this case, the products are planter boxes, ceramic flower pots, and other garden containers, a mini-business which grew out of their pre-retirement hobbies of woodworking and pottery. When these were hobbies, it was not necessary to know how much each pot or planter box cost to make, but when they decided to go into business, the partners wanted to make sure they were charging enough to cover their costs.

Ted's pots were made from clay and were glazed, and by figuring out how many pots could be made from a bag of clay and a jar of glaze, he was able to determine how much each pot cost. Harvey followed a similar procedure in calculating how many boxes of a particular size could be made from $50 worth of lumber. He then added in the cost of the nails.

A few service businesses supply products as part of the service being performed. A bicycle repairer, for example, might need to keep a stock of spokes, chains and other small parts. The customer is then charged both for the time required to make the repair and for the parts needed. Other service businesses, such as tutoring, rubbish hauling, or plant care, have no expenses that fall into the category "cost of goods sold."

Operating Expenses or Overhead. This includes all the other costs involved in running a business--telephone bills, advertising, maintaining equipment, insurance, and so on. Some of these expenses may vary a bit according to how much business you are doing (for example, your telephone bill may be slightly higher in months when business is booming), but they cannot be directly attached to the cost of providing a particular product. Basically, they are the expenses that are necessary to keep yourself "in business," regardless of whether you are selling a lot or a little.

The overhead expenses of home-based mini-businesses are often quite low. This is desirable from several points of view. First, it is a comfort to know that it is not necessary to do a great deal of business in order to break even. Second, it makes it possible to charge lower prices. Just like a giant warehouse or a shop in the "low-rent" district of town, the home-based business can advertise the savings that result from its having "low overhead."

It is important to estimate what your operating expenses will be so that you can figure this into the price you charge for your product or service. **Exercise 10** provides a method for you to use in calculating your probable overhead costs.

Profit. Suppose you have sold 100 hot dogs or 100 planter boxes or been paid for repairing 100 bicycles or hauling 100 loads of rubbish to the dump. From the money you have earned you must pay for the cost of your goods (hot dogs, planter boxes or bicycle parts) and your overhead. Whatever is left over is your profit. This is the money you can "take home" as payment for the time you have spent running the business.

For some people the word "profit" has a negative connotation. This is understandable in a society where too many businesses put big profits ahead of all other human values, such as decent treatment of employees, honest dealings with customers, and preserving the environment. Unfortunately, most small business literature encourages this overly materialistic attitude with such advice as: "The goal in setting prices is to *maximize profits*."

Rather than maximizing profits, it is better to think in terms of making a *fair profit*. Those who care about the social consequences of their work activities may sometimes choose to exchange a high profit for other types of satisfaction. But this does not mean that profit, by itself, is bad. The term is a neutral one, and signifies nothing more than the difference between income and expenses.

Some seniors don't care if they make a profit or not; they have started mini-businesses in order to stay actively involved in their communities and to enjoy themselves, and they view any extra money they may earn as a bonus. Others depend on the profits of their mini-businesses to help pay their living expenses. If you are counting on making a profit, you will need to keep this in mind in deciding how much to charge.

One consideration in determining how much profit is appropriate is the amount of time it takes to manufacture your product or provide your service. A delicately hand-knotted watchband may require very little in the way of materials, but many hours of close attention on the part of the craftsperson. A leather watchband can be made much more rapidly. Since the leatherworker can produce several watchbands in the same time that the macrame artist completes one, most people would agree that the profit on the more delicate object should be higher.

Similarly, in some service businesses, it is customary to charge by the job rather than to set an hourly rate of pay. For example, Carlos, a housepainter, tells his customers in advance what it will cost for him to paint their houses. In order to make a fair profit, Carlos must be able to estimate about how long each job will take.

Other Considerations in Setting Prices

Unfortunately, deciding how much to charge is not as simple as figuring out your costs and adding in the amount of profit you'd like to make. Among the other factors that influence prices are the following:

What Others Charge for Comparable Products or Services. If all the other gardeners in town charge $10 an hour and you ask $20, you are unlikely to get much business--unless you work twice as fast, are able to come on very short notice, have special horticultural expertise, or in some other way can justify the higher price. So one of the things you'll want to do before settling on a price is to look into what others are charging. Oftentimes your product or service won't be exactly the same as theirs, but their prices can still serve as guidelines. For example, Jeannette uses only real butter and cream in her homemade candies, so she knows she can charge more than Dora's Dainties, which uses vegetable shortening and artificial flavorings.

What Customers Are Able and Willing to Pay. This does not mean the same as "what the market will bear." An exploitative approach to pricing such as this has no place in the thinking of socially conscious businesspeople. The concept refers instead to the fact that customer perceptions of value must be taken into account in deciding how much to charge. Margaret's home-baked breads and rolls can serve as an example.

Most of Margaret's neighbors now buy factory-made bread at the supermarket. Margaret knew she would have to charge considerably more for her bread, but that her baked goods would taste a lot better and be fresher and healthier. How much more would her neighbors be willing to pay to have the better bread?

Margaret answered this question by conducting a "market research" study. She gave samples of her bread to some neighbors and asked them how often they would buy her bread if she charged $1.25 a loaf, $1.35, $1.50 and so on. She found that in her neighborhood people really cared about having good, fresh bread, and were willing to pay quite a lot to have it delivered to their doors daily. In another part of town, the answer may have been different; for example, poorer families would probably be more concerned with saving money than having a tastier bread.

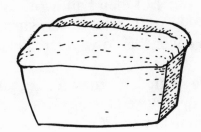

How Much Business You Want to Do. Some mini-businesses set relatively low prices as a way of attracting more customers. This is a good plan so long as the increased volume of business makes up for the smaller profit made on each item. Otherwise the result could be more work for less money.

High prices may discourage sales, and this strategy is often followed by seniors who want to limit the amount of time they put into their mini-businesses. When Herb first began his sign-making business, his low prices and quality workmanship brought him many customers. Soon he found that he had to put in more than 40 hours a week to fill all his orders on time. This was not his idea of retirement! In order to work fewer hours, Herb could simply have turned down some jobs, but he chose instead to raise his prices to the point where he now gets just enough work to keep him busy a comfortable 15-20 hours a week.

The Image You Want Your Business to Have. High prices suggest quality and luxury, low prices suggest economy. In service businesses, a relatively high price may sometimes be necessary to convey a professional image. For example, upon her retirement from a computer company, Helen turned her life-long hobby of interior decorating into a mini-business. She did not supply any furnishings or materials herself, only plans and advice, and her overhead costs were low. Thus, Helen could have made a profit by charging $5 an hour or even less. But she knew that her clients would not value her expertise if she asked so little. Further, people who hire an interior decorator are seldom attempting to economize. Helen felt that her prices should reflect these considerations.

Whether You Expect to Provide Discounts, or sell any of your products at wholesale prices, and if so, how much of your business will be at the lower price. Craftspeople oftentimes engage in both "retail" and "wholesale" sales;   some of their business is done at fairs where customers buy directly from them, while other of their handwork is sold to shops. The price to the shop must ordinarily be quite a lot lower, since shopowners have to mark items up in order to cover their own overhead costs and profit.

What Seems Fair to You. This may reflect your evaluation of what you believe your product or service is really worth, or your knowledge of the financial situation of your customers. On the first point, a beginner may decide to charge less than the "going rate" for a particular service because he knows that it will be necessary to work more slowly and carefully in order to complete the job satisfactorily. Similarly, a craftsperson who gets a bargain on materials may pass the savings on to her customers because it seems the fair thing to do.

Many mini-businesses also take the financial situations of their customers into account in setting their prices. Frank and Maureen are a husband-and-wife housecleaning team. Among their clients are several elderly people on limited incomes who are unable to do their own weekly cleaning. These few clients are charged half of what the ordinary middle-income householder pays. Similarly, Ann is a writer/editor who chooses to do most of her work for small non-profit organizations and political causes she believes in. She charges these groups considerably less than the "going rate" because they can't afford much and because this is her way of contributing to the good work they are doing.

Deciding How Much to Charge

Deciding how much to charge is not an exact science, and it is quite usual for beginning businesspeople to charge too much or too little. Some careful research and thinking at the beginning will help you get off on the right foot, and that is the purpose of **Exercise 11**. But you will probably find that you need to make some adjustments in your prices as time goes on. Do not be dismayed if this happens. In pricing, as in other aspects of your business, you will learn by doing and your skills will grow with experience.

For More Information

"The Management of Prices," Chapter 12 of THE SMALL BUSINESS HANDBOOK, by Irving Burstiner. Prentice-Hall, Englewood Cliffs, NJ, 1979.

Clear explanation of such concepts as "break-even" and "mark-up," along with sound advice on pricing strategies. Particularly useful for product rather than service businesses.

"Pricing Your Products and Services Profitably" (MA4.014)

A low-cost pamphlet available from the Small Business Administration. For a complete list and ordering information, call your local office of the S.B.A. (look under U.S. Government in the telephone book) or write to P.O. Box 15434, Fort Worth, TX, 76119. Ask for SBA-115A.

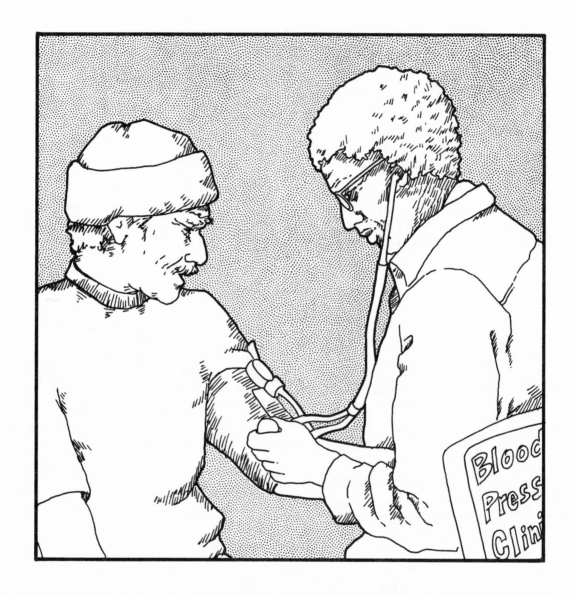

Chapter 6
Spreading the Word

Now that you've taken the initial steps in setting up your business, the next task is to let people know what you have to offer. There are a variety of ways to accomplish this, and many methods are low in cost (or even completely free).

Affordable Advertising

Mini-businesses cannot spend large sums on television advertising or billboards, or even quarter-page ads in the local newspaper. Here are some inexpensive ways to attract customers or clients:

Business Cards. Design one yourself or, if it is important to your business image, engage a graphic artist or an artistically inclined friend to help you select type styles and perhaps add a logo or illustration. Aim for an eye-catching but simple design that reflects the nature of your business. A freelance accountant would probably choose to avoid a bright color or humorous illustration, whereas these might be ideal for a group of women who plan children's parties.

Some examples of effective business cards are shown in Figure 1 on the next page. Note the variety of typefaces and layouts used. The colors of these cards cannot be shown here, but are also quite varied. For example, Aurora Landscaping uses dark blue ink on an off-white background; the T.A.B. Doll Factory card is bright yellow. Which of these cards comes closest to the style you would choose for your mini-business?

Once you have your cards, distribute them widely. Tack them on bulletin boards, give them to friends, and leave small stacks of them in appropriate locations. Carry a supply with you at all times; you never know when one might be needed.

Business Stationery. Many mini-businesses get by without printed letterhead or envelopes. But if you plan to send either personal or form letters to potential clients, or engage in regular correspondence of any type, your

CABINET SHOP
CUSTOM CABINETS
AT GENERIC PRICES

KITCHENS
VANITIES
WOOD TOPS
FINISHING
SHOJI SCREENS
JAPANESE INTERIOR DESIGN

JIM & DAN
361-9927   361-1244

IN SIGHTS
Tours & Consulting

**karen nelson
vicki gala**

(408) 288-9928

**James Langford
Lamp Collector**

1657 Highland Blvd.
Hayward, California
581-6394

Aurora Landscaping
PATRICK A. FERRIS

745 Parma Way
Los Altos
94022

(415) 948-0277

LIC NO. 381068

Cottage Farm Rug Works
Handwoven

Nancy van Nooten
(707) 762-7846

296 Wetmore Lane
Petaluma, CA 94952

Susan Cronin-Paris

Graphic Design and Illustration

368 McKendry Drive
Menlo Park, California 94025

(415) 327-5199

"T.A.B. DOLL
FACTORY"
540 MENKER
SAN JOSE, CALIF.
U.S.A. 95128
(408)293-0104

RICK & TERRI
BALANDRA

"RAGGIES"

Figure 1. Business Cards

image will be much more professional and businesslike if you have your own stationery. Your stationery can be printed at the same time, and by the same person, as your business card. And if you have a logo designed for one, it can easily be included on the other. Your stationery itself then becomes a form of advertising.

3x5 or 4x6 Cards. Your business card will give the name and nature of your business, your address and telephone number, and perhaps an additional short phrase ("24-hour service"). If you have more to tell, or if you have decided to do without business cards for the time being, consider the use of 3x5 or 4x6 cards. Neatly hand-lettered or typed, these can be posted on supermarket bulletin boards and other appropriate locations.

If you plan to distribute your cards widely, save time by having them photocopied. An 8-1/2 x 11 sheet of paper can be penciled into four segments, each approximately 4x6 in size, or six segments of approximately 3x5. You need only repeat your message four or six times and have the results copied onto lightweight cardboard ("cardstock"). Selecting a color other than white will help your card stand out, and the use of a paper cutter will result in a neat trim. Keep track of where your cards are posted and check back occasionally to make sure they are still in place and easily visible.

Flyers. This is a good way to tell your neighbors about a new service business--gardening, odd jobs, housesitting and so on. Even amateurs can usually produce a satisfactory flyer. Do a "mock-up" first, figuring out just what you want to say and how your information will look best on the page. Typing and the careful use of rub-down letters (such as Letraset or Zipatone) will give a more professional look to your flyer, but hand lettering works well too. An illustration, perhaps a line drawing clipped from an old magazine, will add interest. Then take your "camera-ready art work" to a photocopy or quick-print shop, select a cheerful color, and have several hundred copies made.

Postal regulations forbid putting anything other than U.S. mail in mailboxes, so distribute your flyers by tucking them inside screen doors or under doormats. If your area is a large one and you don't feel up to delivering all the flyers yourself, hire a responsible teenager or recruit a younger relative. Save some of your flyers to post on bulletin boards and pass out or mail to friends.

Flyers are also useful to announce special events. Joanne, an energetic 59-year old woman, and four of her talented friends hold a yearly crafts bazaar, just after Thanksgiving. Here they sell the array of well-made pottery, fabric art, and other items they have created during the year. Held in the spacious home of one of the group members, the bazaar is an elegant affair, with catered refreshments, holiday decorations, and live music.

Flyers announcing this event are, in this case, professionally designed and distributed. They are posted on bulletin boards and kiosks and in store windows throughout the city. They are also mailed to all previous customers. This is the only form of advertising the women do, and it is very successful in attracting holiday shoppers in search of unique gifts.

Direct Mail. This term includes postcards, letters, flyers, catalogs and anything else that is mailed directly to the people you want to reach. Oftentimes discarded as "junk mail," your piece will be more favorably received if sent to a carefully selected list of people who are most likely to want to know about your mini-business. These might be people who are interested in you as a person, such as your friends, neighbors, fellow church and club members, and former work associates. Or they might be people who have special need of the service you are offering--dog owners if you teach canine obedience training, bicyclists for the handyman who specializes in bicycle repair, retail stores and homeowners for a window washing service.

The trick, then, is to find a listing of the names and addresses of such people. A little detective work may be required. For example, where would you look for a listing of the bicyclists in your town? Possibilities include the membership list of a bicycle club, city hall records of people who have taken out bicycle licenses, the customer lists of new and used bicycle sales shops (if they don't have their own repair departments). Can you think of other ways to locate potential users of a bicycle repair service?

Almost all mini-businesses use direct mail on occasion--for example, sending a postcard to a small group of friends to let them know you are in business. Others make extensive use of this type of advertising. If you are among those who plan to use direct mail on a regular basis, consult the post office about special rates for bulk mailing, and be sure to do more reading and research about the most effective ways to use direct mail. The books listed at the end of the chapter are a good place to begin.

Referrals (Word-of-Mouth). A satisfied customer or client who tells his or her friends about your excellent service or attractive product is by far the best form of advertising. But referrals can also be solicited. For example, Jerry and May decided to provide after-school care for primary-age children because they both enjoy boys and girls of this age, because this mini-business would allow them time flexibility during the better part of the day, and because they knew that the existing child care centers in town served only pre-schoolers. The couple called on the directors of all these centers, explaining their qualifications and rates, and asked that inquiring parents of older children be referred to them. This proved to be their most effective form of "advertising."

Personal Contact. In many instances, the best way to let people know about your mini-business is to tell them about it yourself, by either telephoning or calling on them in person. This is the method used by Harold, Ed and Martha to spread the word of their "shop-sitting" service. As retired retailers themselves, these three friends knew that owners of small stores are often reluctant to take even short vacations, not wanting either to close up the business and thereby inconvenience regular customers or to leave it in the hands of inexperienced friends or relatives. Knowledgeable "shop-sitters" could keep a business functioning effectively in the owner's absence.

Among them, the three partners knew quite a few of the shop-owners in town, and these they simply telephoned to announce their new service. The others they called on personally, selecting a time when the owner wasn't busy with customers. Their only written material was a one-page typewritten statement of their rates, their qualifications, and the names of several references, which was left with potential clients after the conversation. This was useful backup, but it was the personal contact itself that actually communicated their message.

Portfolio. This is not so much a separate form of advertising as a visual aid to be used when calling on potential customers, or to show to people who have heard of your mini-business from some other source but need to see examples of what you can do before deciding to use your service. A graphic artist, for example, might collect a representative sampling of flyers, brochures and invitations he has designed, or a photographer may select some of her favorite pictures.

On the other hand, not everyone can carry actual samples of their work with them. If you are a stained glass artist, sign-maker, cake decorator, rug-braider, playground equipment manufacturer, or muralist, you will need some other means of displaying your expertise. In such instances, color snapshots of some of your best work, arranged behind clear plastic sheets in a small scrapbook or photo album, will make an impressive portfolio.

Some service businesses also use portfolios. Marianne, a retired dancer, teaches ballet, tap, ballroom and jazz dance to small groups of children in a studio which she converted from her double garage. Recitals are held in a school auditorium, and a portfolio made up of color photographs of these events is useful to parents who want to see what Marianne's students have accomplished.

In addition to samples of your work, a portfolio may include your resume, letters from satisfied customers, clippings of newspaper articles about your mini-business, and anything else that you think will help you put your best foot forward.

Newspapers. The choice here is between classified ("want ads") and small display ads in other parts of the paper.

Classified ads can be surprisingly effective. People who read the want ads are usually already in a buying mood. They know they need a carpenter or a place to board their cat, and are simply looking for a good one. The person behind the classifieds desk at your local paper can often help you put together an attractive and economical ad. Figure 2, on the next page, shows the variety of ways housecleaning services advertise in the classified section of one local paper. Which one do you think has spent its money most effectively?

Since people usually discard their newspaper as soon as they have read it, classified ads have to run in just about every issue of the paper. This cost can add up after awhile. Here is an instance where it will pay to keep careful track of how customers learn of your service. If a large number of people see and

Figure 2. Classified Ads

Figure 3. Display Ads

respond to your classified ad, you will know your money is well spent. If only a few come because of the ad, you will probably want to discontinue it.

The chief advantage of a display ad is that it is placed among the regular news stories, so that people who aren't actively seeking out your type of service will still see what you have to offer. Further, it may be possible to place your ad in a section of the paper whose readers will be particularly attuned to your type of business, for example, the travel pages for a travel service or guidebook, or the "kitchen" section for food-related products.

Ordinarily, mini-businesses find display ads too costly in relation to the number of customers they attract. This is because even very small and simple ads, such as the one for Maid-for-a-Day (Figure 3), must be especially typeset. Moreover, the rates for running display ads are usually higher than for classifieds. But the women who operate Maid-for-a-Day decided it was worth taking a chance on this expenditure. They were right; the clever name of their mini-business attracted the attention of numerous readers, and they received many calls as a result. Seaside Lock and Key is another example of an effective small display ad.

One form of display advertising that can be relatively economical is reproducing your business card This is less costly because the ad need not be separately designed and because newspapers often have special sections for these ads and offer them at special rates. Not all newspapers follow this practice, however; it is more common among small weeklies and trade publications than large general circulation newspapers.

If you plan to use this method of advertising, keep your dual purpose in mind when ordering your business cards. Make sure the design is one that will reproduce well and that you have included enough information to make the card effective as a newspaper ad.

Yellow Pages. Some types of mini-businesses find the yellow pages of the telephone book an essential form of advertising; for others this is a waste of money. Examine your own yellow pages to see what types of businesses are listed there. Then ask yourself: If I were new in town and needed a *(substitute your type of business)*, would I consult the yellow pages to find one? As an example, most people would answer "yes" in the case of a washing-machine repairer, but "no" for a marriage counselor. If you do decide to advertise in the yellow pages, it is often worth the additional cost of having your listing printed in bold face type, or even using a small display ad.

Signs. Municipal zoning regulations usually limit the size and type of exterior signs permitted in residential neighborhoods, but rarely are they completely forbidden. An attractive sign can inform passers-by of the interesting mini-business being conducted within. (Check with your local planning department to learn what is acceptable in your town or county.)

If you sell at fairs or conferences, you will probably also want a sign that can be attached to the front of your table or booth, or placed on an easel by your side. You can make these yourself using stencils or press-down vinyl letters, but if your talent in these areas is limited, it may pay to have a sign professionally done or to enlist the assistance of a more experienced friend.

Customer Gifts. Pencils, balloons, matchbooks, keyrings and a host of other small items can be imprinted with the name, address and telephone number of your mini-business and distributed to customers and the general public. This is an especially appropriate means of advertising when the item reflects the nature of your business--pencils for a secretarial service or keyrings for someone who does minor repairs on automobiles. Look in your yellow pages under "Advertising Specialties" for the names of firms who do this kind of work.

Brochures. Brochures are not often used by mini-businesses, but some types of service business find them essential. A tutoring center, for example, might use a brochure to describe the various subjects taught, qualifications of the tutors, rates and so on. These could be mailed to inquiring parents, as well as distributed to school counselors and teachers.

Brochures come in all sizes and shapes; one of the most common is made from an 8-1/2 x 11 sheet of heavyweight paper folded in thirds to give a finished piece that is 8-1/2 inches high and slightly less than 4 inches wide. It is possible to make such a brochure yourself, using typed copy, rub-off letters, and simple graphics, but people who use brochures are more likely to want one that is professionally designed and typeset. If you choose to hire a graphic artist, be sure to clearly specify how much you want to spend, since the cost of brochures varies widely.

Other Ideas. Other advertising possibilities include local magazines, regional or national special interest magazines, trade shows, directory listings, slide shows, demonstrations, and free samples. Consult the reference works listed at the end of the chapter to learn more about these types of advertising.

Cooperative Advertising. A good way to save advertising dollars is to join forces with other mini-businesses. A teen-ager hired to deliver your flyer from door-to-door might carry along two or three others for only a slight additional charge. Several child care centers in different parts of town could combine to publish one newspaper ad. Craftspeople with different specialties can refer potential customers to one another. The advantage of this kind of cooperation is not only in the time and money saved; friendly support networks make being in business much more fun.

A Special Note on Mail Order: Unlike mini-businesses that serve local customers, selling by mail requires extensive advertising. This can be very costly if not carefully planned and monitored. Because of the importance of paid advertising in the field of mail order, the subject cannot be covered adequately in these pages. Some good books on the subject are listed at the end of the chapter. You may also want to consult a S.C.O.R.E. counselor (see "Where to Get Help" in Chapter 11).

Free Publicity

Publicity refers to the attention that is attracted to your mini-business because it is newsworthy or because you are known in your community. Many businesses get along without any form of paid advertising and rely entirely on free publicity to bring them customers. Here are some ways to publicize your mini-business:

Newspaper Articles. Your business idea may be so novel, or your local weekly so hungry for news, that reporters begin telephoning as soon as you "hang out your shingle." More often, you will need to take the initiative. The best way to do this is to send a "press release" to the relevant newspapers in your area.

A press release is a one- or two-page double-spaced article written as if you were a reporter. Use your business stationery. At the top of the first page, type the date, FOR IMMEDIATE RELEASE, and your name and telephone number. Make your story easy-to-read, factual and, above all, newsworthy. Look for what is unique and interesting about your mini-business, or tie your activities to something else that is happening in the news.

Does your business respond to a particularly pressing community need, for example, grocery delivery to the housebound elderly? Is it unusual to find seniors undertaking the kind of business you are operating--giving windsurfing lessons or playing in a rock band? If a prolonged hot spell is making local news, might it not be a good time for an article about your handcrafted porch swings? Or during Senior Citizen or Small Business Weeks, what could be more interesting than a story about imaginative seniors who are supplementing their retirement incomes and having a good time by operating mini-businesses?

In addition to sending press releases, you can invite reporters to attend special events or performances you have organized (send them free tickets), or simply telephone them with your news and encourage them to interview you in person. These techniques work best in smaller communities.

If you do receive newspaper publicity, be sure to cut out the article and have photocopies made. You can send these, along with a cover letter, to potential customers. Or you can use quotes from the article in a flyer or ad. The publicity itself will bring you lots of customers, but you can make it work for you in these other ways too.

Television and Radio. Have you ever imagined yourself as a media personality? Obtaining radio or T.V. coverage is not as difficult as you may think. Send information about your mini-business to local stations, suggesting that it would be a good subject for a human interest news feature or a segment on a "magazine"-type show. Volunteer to be on a talk show or to organize a panel of retirees representing a variety of mini-businesses. As with newspaper articles, tying your activities to other news events will increase the likelihood that you will receive television or radio publicity.

Demonstrating Your Expertise. You can make yourself known by giving talks or teaching classes on subjects that relate to your mini-business. An accountant might speak to a civic group on commonly overlooked tax deductions, or a caterer teach an adult school class on making holiday cookies. You would not use such an occasion to "sell" your mini-business, but of course would have a supply of business cards to give to anyone who expressed interest. (Activities such as these may also attract news coverage, spreading the word even further.)

Writing newspaper or magazine articles or columns is another means of demonstrating your expertise and making yourself known. Ruth and Annette, for example, who operate a travel service for retirees, write a regular travel column for the Senior Gazette, a newspaper distributed through nearly 25 senior centers in a three county region.

Community Participation. Donating your time or product to a worthy cause often brings additional business as well as the good feeling of contributing to one's community. For example, Helen and Maggie, whose business is selling arrangements of the fresh flowers they grow in their large suburban gardens, donated the floral centerpieces for an appreciation luncheon for hospital volunteers. Subsequently, many of the volunteers asked the two women to supply flowers for their own parties and family events.

Even participation in community activities that are unrelated to your mini-business is a way to meet people who may someday have occasion to purchase your product or service. It would be a mistake to join clubs or volunteer your time solely in order to make business contacts. Your insincerity will undoubtedly be felt. But this can be an extra added push to get out and become involved in the life-enriching undertaking of serving your community and learning to know your fellow citizens.

Deciding How to Spread the Word

Having reviewed the range of advertising and publicity options available to mini-businesses, you are now ready to decide how to begin spreading the word. **Exercise 12** provides a format for evaluating these choices. For your type of business, is the method appropriate? (consistent with your image? likely to be seen by potential customers? likely to be regarded favorably by them?) Is it affordable? And perhaps most important, will it be enjoyable? There is no sense in planning to give talks if you are terrified of appearing before an audience. On the other hand, if you are a ham at heart, you may decide to do a great many talks even if you think this will not be your most efficient means of spreading the word. Another thing to keep in mind: part of the fun of running a mini-business is the opportunity it provides to learn new skills and meet new challenges. Your need to find customers or clients may provide the motivation to explore some new ways of expressing yourself.

For More Information

Advertising and Publicity, General

HOW TO PROMOTE YOUR OWN BUSINESS, by Gary Blake and Robert Bly. New American Library, New York, NY, 1983.
An extremely useful book of information on low cost methods of advertising and publicity.

THE SECRETS OF PRACTICAL MARKETING FOR SMALL BUSINESS, by Herman R. Holtz. Prentice-Hall, Inc., Englewood Cliffs, NY, 1982.
Excellent overview of this important topic.

MARKETING WITHOUT ADVERTISING, by Michael Phillips and Salli Rasberry. Nolo Press, Berkeley, CA, 1986.
A thorough , easy to read discussion of ways to build "word-of-mouth" recommendations for your small business.

"Marketing Small Business," SMALL BUSINESS REPORTER (SBR-203)
Succinctly covers many aspects of marketing, from research to advertising and budgeting. Available at Bank of America branches in California, or write to the Bank of America, Department 3120, P.O. Box 37000, San Francisco, CA, 94137, for mail order information.

Mail Order Advertising

MAIL ORDER MOONLIGHTING, Revised Edition, by Cecil C. Hoge. Ten Speed Press, Berkeley, CA, 1988.

MONEY IN YOUR MAILBOX: HOW TO START AND OPERATE A MAIL ORDER BUSINESS, by L. Perry Wilbur. John Wiley & Sons, New York, NY, 1985.

"Selling by Mail Order" (MA4.023). Available from Small Business Administration, P.O. Box 15434, Fort Worth, TX, 76119.

Chapter 7
Keeping Records

Once your business is underway, you will need some method for keeping track of your finances. Far too many mini-businesspeople shy away from "paperwork." Some are afraid they will find the subject too confusing and so just muddle along, hoping everything will turn out all right. Others think that because their goal is to provide a needed community service rather than make a profit, they need not concern themselves with money matters. Or they believe that, because their business is small, they can keep all the information in their head. This is a mistake. Organized written records are essential for even the smallest of small scale businesses. Here's why.

First, you will need to make reports to the government in the form of tax returns, sales tax remittances, and so on. These can be completed much more quickly and painlessly if the relevant figures are at your fingertips. Careful record-keeping will probably save you tax-money too.

Second, and of even greater importance, good records will provide you with the information you need to make sound business decisions. As has already been touched upon in Chapter 5, long-run business success depends on the apparently obvious principle of taking in more money than you are spending. Yet, without adequate financial records, it is easy to be misled about the actual costs of keeping your doors open. Even when sales are brisk, a mini-business can lose money if expenses are not carefully monitored. With a good set of records, you will not fall into this trap. You will know just what your financial situation is, and if you are losing money, you will have the basis for deciding whether you should try to get more customers, raise your prices, or cut back on expenses.

Good records need not be complex and detailed. Indeed, the best rule is to make them as simple as possible. This chapter will tell you about a system that has worked for many mini-businesses. It is not the only way to do things, however, so feel free to modify it to suit your own needs.

No matter what method you use, the process of record-keeping will involve three steps: recording financial transactions, summarizing these into categories in an account book, and further summarizing the information into a one-page "profit-and-loss" statement.

Recording Financial Transactions

Financial transactions are of two types--money coming in (income or "revenues") and money going out (expenses). *Income transactions* are usually recorded on sales slips, receipts or invoices, and expenses on the check stubs of your business checkbook.

Sales slips are most commonly used when someone purchases your product and pays you at the time of the sale. This form records the date, the type of item purchased, and the amount paid, including sales tax. An example of a completed sales slip is shown in Figure 4.

People who perform a service (rather than sell a product) typically use a receipt instead of a sales slip, as in Figure 5.

If you need to bill your customers or clients for your product or services, invoicing is the preferred method (see Figure 6). Keep all unpaid invoices in a file folder labeled "Invoices Outstanding." When the payment comes in, note the date and amount on the invoice, and transfer it to an "Invoices Paid" file. Businesses that have a relatively small number of customers and a large number of transactions with each of them usually have an "Invoices Paid" file for each customer.

Booklets of blank sales slips, receipts and invoices are all available at low cost from stationery and office supply stores. All three of these forms are similar in that they supply an original, usually white, which is given to the customer, and a carbon copy, usually yellow, which you retain for your records.

Keeping track of *expense transactions* is just as easy. When you receive a bill for supplies, materials or anything else you have ordered, circle the due date in red and put it in a file folder called "Bills To Be Paid." Pay all your bills with your business checking account, and note carefully on the check stub or check register the person or company to whom the check was written, the amount, and what the money was for. On the bill itself, write down the date paid and check number, and file it in a "Bills Paid" folder. Again, if you do business with a relatively small number of accounts, you may want to have a "Bills Paid" file for each. That's all there is to it.

Sold By Fred Date Oct 22 19—

Name

Address

REG. NO.		AMT. REC'D	ACCT. FWD.
	1		
1	2	T-shirt	7 95
1	3	Matching shorts	9 95
	4		
	5		17 90
	6	tax (6%)	1 07
	7		
	8		18 97
	9		
	10		
	11		
	12		
	13		
	14	30	

5A200 REDIFORM®

Figure 4. Sales Slip

DATE July 27 19 — NO. 9446

RECEIVED OF Angela Truzzi

ADDRESS

$ 10.00

FOR housecleaning services

HOW PAID: check

BALANCE DUE

BY Hank Fisher

8K826 REDIFORM®

Figure 5. Receipt

INVOICE

WORKWAYS CONSULTING GROUP
61 Park Avenue
Redwood City, CA 94062

INVOICE NO. 2057

SOLD TO			SHIPPED TO		
Tech-Top Computers			same		
STREET & NO			STREET & NO		
345 Westview Drive					
CITY	STATE	ZIP	CITY	STATE	ZIP
Sunnyvale	CA	94763			

CUSTOMER'S ORDER	SALESMAN	TERMS	F O B	DATE
Nov 21, —		30 days		Dec 13, —

1	Worker Participation Resource Guide			14	00
12	Worker Participation: Tipsheet	1	00	12	00
	Total Materials			26	00
	Tax on Materials (6½%)			1	69
2 hrs	Consulting Services	35	00	70	00
	Total Due			97	69

REDIFORM® 7H 722

Figure 6. Invoice

Summarizing Transactions in Ledgers

A "ledger" is nothing more than a sheet of lined paper with columns that allows you to enter your income and expenses by category. You can purchase pads of ledger paper in a stationery store.

The ledgers shown in Figures 7 and 8 belong to Cookie Cut-Ups, Harley and Donna's mini-business of manufacturing unique cookie cutters. Some of these are sold directly to customers and some to kitchenware stores.

Harley and Donna usually enter figures into their *income ledger* once a week, or more often if they have had a lot of transactions. This is also when they deposit the money into their business checking account.

Using their sales slips, they total up all of the money (cash and checks) they have received from individual purchasers. This is divided according to the amount that was paid for the cookie cutters themselves and the amount that covers the sales tax. The former is written down under "Taxable Sales" and the latter under "Sales Tax." Sometimes individual customers order special cookie cutters by mail, and they are charged $1.00 extra to cover the cost of postage. This money is entered in a separate column.

Finally, sales to kitchenware stores are entered in the column headed "Wholesale." Usually the merchandise going to stores has to be mailed, so Cookie Cut-Ups collects postage money from these customers too. Wholesale customers do not pay sales tax.

In the last column, "Total," Harley and Donna have added up all the money they took in over the week. Then, at the end of the month, each column is totaled to provide a summary of their monthly income.

You may choose to do things a bit differently from Harley and Donna. For example, if you have several different types of products or services, you may want to have a column for each one. The idea is simply to have a summary of the total amount of money taken in, divided into whatever categories will be most helpful to you.

A portion of Harley and Donna's *expense ledger* is shown in Figure 8. They have transferred the information from their business checkbook to

1	2	3	4	5	6	7
		Taxable Sales	Sales Tax	Wholesale Sales	Postage	TOTAL
Date	Sales Period					

INCOME LEDGER Month of <u>July</u>

Date	Sales Period	Taxable Sales	Sales Tax	Wholesale Sales	Postage	TOTAL
1						
2						
3						
4						
5						
6						
7	July 1-7	210 —	12 60		2 —	224 60
8						
9	July 8-9			127 —	7 20	134 20
10						
11						
12						
13						
14	July 10-14	355 —	21 30		12 —	388 30
15–31						
	TOTALS FOR MONTH					

Adapted from *Small Time Operator*

Figure 7. Income Ledger

EXPENDITURE LEDGER

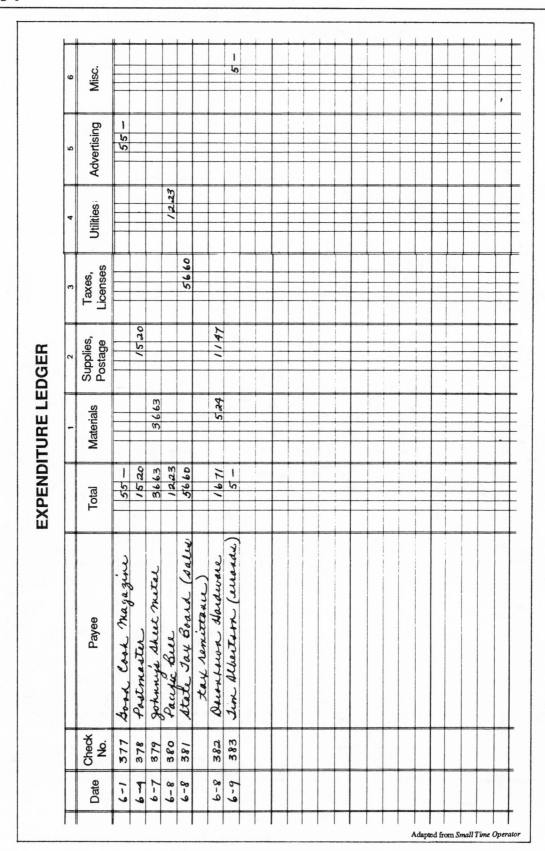

Date	Check No.	Payee	Total	1 Materials	2 Supplies, Postage	3 Taxes, Licenses	4 Utilities	5 Advertising	6 Misc.
6-1	377	Good Cook Magazine	55 —					55 —	
6-7	378	Postmaster	1520		1520				
6-7	379	Johnny's Sheet Metal	3663	3663					
6-8	380	Pacific Bell	1223				1223		
6-8	381	State Tax Board (sales tax remittance)	5660			5660			
6-8	382	Downtown Hardware	1671	524	1147				
6-9	383	Jim Alberton (award)	5 —						5 —

Adapted from *Small Time Operator*

Figure 8. Expenditure Ledger

organize the figures into categories. The first of these, "Materials," refers to the things that go into the manufacture of their cookie cutters--tin, solder, flux and rivets. All of the other categories represent overhead expenses. (These are the types of expenses that Harley and Donna thought they would have most frequently. Your categories might be different.)

For the most part, the entries in this expense ledger are self-explanatory. Note two special cases. Check #380, written to the telephone company, covers only a portion of Harley and Donna's monthly bill--the part that is related to the cost of operating their mini-business. The rest of the bill, covering their personal calls, is paid for with their personal checking account. Check #382, to the hardware store, paid for a variety of small purchases. Most of these were office supplies, but one was a roll of solder. The total expense is therefore broken down into two categories, the cost of the solder being entered under "Materials" and the remainder under "Supplies."

As with the income ledger, the columns in the expense ledger will be added up at the end of the month. Harley and Donna will then know what the costs of operating their business have been.

Drawing Up a Profit-and-Loss Statement

A profit-and-loss statement sometimes goes by other names, such as "income statement" or "operating statement." Its most common nickname is "P-and-L." These all refer to the same thing--a summary of how the money going out compares with the money coming in. Profit-and-loss statements are usually drawn up at the end of each month, and then totaled at the end of the year.

Grandma's Attic is a used toy exchange run by two real grandmothers, Lucy and Mildred. They purchase outgrown toys and games and resell them to economical parents and child care centers. Their pricing policy is a simple one: they charge twice what they paid for the item.

Figure 9, on the next page, shows a slightly simplified version of one of their monthly profit-and-loss statements. Their *total income* for this month, listed first, was $600. The *cost of goods sold* was easy for them to calculate, because they know that each toy costs them half of what it sells for. Half of

```
                    PROFIT-AND-LOSS STATEMENT

                         GRANDMA'S ATTIC
                           JUNE 19--


    Total Income                                    $600

    Cost of Goods Sold                             <300>

    Gross Profit                                    300

    Operating Expenses
         Advertising               25
         Telephone                 10
         Supplies                   5
         Other                     10

         Total                                     <50>


    Net Profit                                     $250
```

Figure 9. Profit-and-Loss Statement

$600 is $300. This means that their *gross profit*, found by subtracting cost of goods sold from total income, was also $300. (Other types of businesses may have to take more factors into account in determining cost of goods sold, as discussed in Chapter 5. A service business has no such costs; its total income is the same as its gross profit.)

Lucy and Mildred then totaled their monthly overhead or *operating expenses*, found in their expense ledger, and subtracted this from their gross profit. The result, $250, was their *net profit*, the amount they could divide up in payment for their month's work.

The two women felt quite satisfied with this return. When they first started out, sales were slow, and their operating expenses added up to more than their gross profit. This meant they were operating at a *loss*. Their first month's loss was $65 and, following conventional bookkeeping notation, was written on their statement as follows: <$65>. (Whenever negative numbers appear in ledgers or on profit-and-loss statements, they are surrounded by parentheses or brackets.)

When the "bottom line" of a profit-and-loss statement shows a loss, the business is said to be operating "in the red." This figure of speech is left over from the days when losses were recorded in red ink--a clear sign of danger! Operating at a loss, however, is quite normal for beginning businesses. Do you think your own mini-business will operate "in the red" during its early months? How long do you anticipate it will take until you are "in the black?"

Drawing up a profit-and-loss statement each month is an important way to keep track of just how your business is doing. You can compare monthly figures for much more than the "bottom line." For example, do your monthly sales (total income) fluctuate markedly? If so, perhaps your business is a seasonal one. Knowing that you can expect to do less business during certain months of the year will allow you to plan ahead for these lean times. How do your operating expenses compare from month to month? Are they gradually creeping upward? If so, perhaps they can be trimmed a bit without a loss of sales. With profit-and-loss statements you can do much more than just keep records; these statements allow you to observe your business with a critical eye and plan for its future.

Other Types of Financial Records

Petty Cash. It is a good habit to pay for your business expenses by check whenever practicable. At the same time, you will probably have occasional small expenses that you pay for out-of-pocket. Use of a public telephone to make business calls when you are away from home, a few postage stamps, and a minor purchase at the stationery store are examples.

Keep a small notebook to record petty cash expenditures. For each transaction, note the date, the nature of the purchase, and the amount. Attach the sales receipt if you received one. Then, at the end of the month, total these expenses and reimburse yourself by writing yourself a check from your business checkbook. Enter this transaction in your expenditure ledger by dividing the total amount into appropriate categories (telephone, postage, supplies, and so on).

Automobile Mileage Log. The miles you travel in your car while carrying out business-related activities is a tax-deductible expense. Keep a notebook in the glove compartment to record the date, purpose, and mileage of each business trip. Be sure to note even very short trips, as these add up over a period of time. You need not transfer mileage records to your expenditure ledger until year's end.

Other. Depending on the nature of your mini-business, you may need some other record-keeping systems. If you frequently buy merchandise, materials, or other supplies on credit, an *accounts payable ledger* will keep track of how much you owe and to whom. Similarly, an *accounts receivable ledger* lets you see at a glance the money that others owe you. In businesses involving substantial amounts of materials or merchandise, an *inventory record* provides information about stock on hand so you will know when it's time to reorder. And if you have employees, a *payroll ledger* is a must (see Chapter 10). You can learn more about these systems by consulting the readings listed at the end of the chapter.

A Final Note

There is certainly more you will want to learn about financial record-keeping, but you now have the basics. More detail can be found in the reference works listed below.

Should you hire a bookkeeper to help you keep your records? If you anticipate that you will have a lot of unusual transactions, this may be a good idea, but such an expenditure is ordinarily not necessary. It may be slow going at first, and you will probably have many questions, but you will be surprised at how quickly you will become adept at the process of keeping your own records. You may even come to enjoy it!

For More Information

SMALL TIME OPERATOR: HOW TO START YOUR OWN SMALL BUSINESS, KEEP YOUR BOOKS, PAY YOUR TAXES AND STAY OUT OF TROUBLE, by Bernard Kamoroff. Bell Springs Publishing, Laytonville, CA, revised every year.
> *If you can afford only one other book to help you with your mini-business, this is the one to buy. It explains financial record-keeping, taxation and the various legal aspects of operating a small business.*

"Financial Records for Small Business," SMALL BUSINESS REPORTER (SBR-128)
> *Explains how to set up and keep financial records. Available at Bank of America branches in California or write to the Bank of America, Department 3120, P.O. Box 37000, San Francisco, CA, 94137, for mail order information.*

"Budgeting in a Small Business Firm" (MA1.015), "Recordkeeping in Small Business" (MA1.017)
> *These are low-cost pamphlets available from the Small Business Administration. For a complete list and ordering information, call your local office of the S.B.A. (look under U.S. Government in the telephone book), or write to P.O. Box 15434, Fort Worth, TX, 76119. Ask for SBA-115A.*

Chapter 8
Paying Taxes

Financial record-keeping may eventually become an enjoyable part of your business activity, but in all likelihood, the same cannot be said for paying taxes. This chapter will not attempt to convince you that taxes are fun, nor will it try to teach you all you need to know about computing your taxes and submitting your tax returns. Taxation is a complex subject that needs more detailed treatment than is possible here. What this chapter will do is alert you to some basic facts to help you get off on the right foot. You can learn more from the reading materials listed at the end.

Some people wonder whether it is really necessary to concern themselves with taxes when their businesses are so small. Perhaps they know of mini-businesspeople who do not pay taxes and have never been in any kind of trouble. Why shouldn't they do the same?

It is true that some "small time operators" do not file tax returns or pay taxes on their business income. This is sometimes intentional, more often not. Jack is a case in point. He does odd jobs for people in his neighborhood--mowing lawns, hauling trash, washing windows. He often barters for his services, receiving some homemade jam or firewood or clothing repair instead of money. When he gets cash he simply pockets it and uses it to buy his groceries that week. It doesn't occur to him that he is doing business, and that the goods and money he receives for his work constitute business income. As far as he is concerned, neighbors are simply helping each other out.

As things stand, Jack will probably remain in blissful ignorance, but having read this far, you cannot claim the same for yourself. So make the best of things! Completing tax forms may never be fun, but it can become interesting. As with other aspects of operating your mini-business, taxation provides a new area of knowledge to explore. Furthermore, there may be times when your mini-business will actually *save* you money on your taxes, a happy thought indeed.

Federal Income Tax

As a retired person, you probably have income from social security, a company retirement plan, investments, or some combination of these. You report your income and calculate your federal taxes on I.R.S. Form 1040. As a mini-businessperson you will continue to use Form 1040, simply adding an attachment to record your business-related income and expenses. This attachment, known as Schedule C, is shown in Figure 10.

If you look closely, you will notice that Schedule C bears a striking resemblence to a profit-and-loss statement. Line 1 of Schedule C corresponds to your yearly *total income*. Lines 2 and 3 are your *cost of goods sold* and *gross profit* for the year. Your *overhead* or *operating expenses* are totaled on line 30, and on line 31 you will find your *net profit*.

The only really tricky part in all of this is learning what are legitimate business expenses. This is where the reading materials listed at the end of the chapter will be most helpful. For example, since you are using your home as your place of business, you may be able to claim a portion of your rent or home maintenance costs as business expenses. Similarly, some of your auto expenses may be deductible. Since you owe taxes on your net profit (after subtracting deductible expenses), it pays--literally--to claim every expense you are legally entitled to. Depending on your tax bracket, it may be a good idea to ask an accountant for help in preparing this part of your tax return.

People who have turned a hobby into a mini-business are often pleased to discover that many of the costs attached to pursuing a cherished personal interest have now become tax-deductible as business expenses. Here are some examples: subscriptions to magazines about the hobby, reference books, membership dues in relevant organizations, attending classes and seminars (including the cost of travel, and of lodging when an overnight stay is required), attending trade shows and conventions, some of the expense of entertaining fellow enthusiasts (if related to promoting the hobby-related business), purchase of tools and equipment, repairs of equipment. Indeed, the desire to maintain a relatively costly hobby on a reduced retirement income is one factor motivating some seniors to go into business. Even if your earnings are minimal, the hobby is no longer a financial drain when some expenses can be "written off."

Businesses sometimes operate at a loss, especially when first starting up. Since your business income is combined with all of your other sources of income in calculating the taxes you owe, a business loss will reduce your total tax obligation. Bill and Barbara will serve as an example. They lead bicycle tours for people over 55.

SCHEDULE C
(Form 1040)

Department of the Treasury
Internal Revenue Service √(0)

Profit or (Loss) From Business or Profession
(Sole Proprietorship)
Partnerships, Joint Ventures, etc., Must File Form 1065.
▶ Attach to Form 1040, Form 1041, or Form 1041S.   ▶ See Instructions for Schedule C (Form 1040).

OMB No. 1545-0074

19– –

Attachment
Sequence No. **09**

Name of proprietor	Social security number (SSN)

A Principal business or profession, including product or service (see Instructions)

B Principal business code
(from Part IV) ▶

C Business name and address ▶ ....

D Employer ID number (Not SSN)

E Method(s) used to value closing inventory:
   (1) ☐ Cost   **(2)** ☐ Lower of cost or market   **(3)** ☐ Other (attach explanation)

F Accounting method: **(1)** ☐ Cash   **(2)** ☐ Accrual   **(3)** ☐ Other (specify) ▶ ....

	Yes	No
G Was there any change in determining quantities, costs, or valuations between opening and closing inventory? (If "Yes," attach explanation.)		
H Are you deducting expenses for an office in your home?		
I Did you file **Form 941** for this business for any quarter in 1987?		
J Did you "materially participate" in the operation of this business during 1987? (If "No," see Instructions for limitations on losses.) . . .		
K Was this business in operation at the end of 1987?		
L How many months was this business in operation during 1987? . . . . ▶		

M If this schedule includes a loss, credit, deduction, income, or other tax benefit relating to a tax shelter required to be registered, check here.   ▶ ☐
    If you check this box, you **MUST** attach **Form 8271.**

Part I Income

1a Gross receipts or sales	**1a**	
b Less: Returns and allowances	**1b**	
c Subtract line 1b from line 1a and enter the balance here	**1c**	
2 Cost of goods sold and/or operations (from Part III, line 8)	**2**	
3 Subtract line 2 from line 1c and enter the **gross profit** here	**3**	
4 Other income (including windfall profit tax credit or refund received in 1987). . . .	**4**	
5 Add lines 3 and 4. This is the **gross income** . . . . ▶	**5**	

Part II Deductions

6 Advertising		**23** Repairs		
7 Bad debts from sales or services (see Instructions.)		**24** Supplies (not included in Part III) . .		
8 Bank service charges		**25** Taxes		
9 Car and truck expenses		**26** Travel, meals, and entertainment:		
10 Commissions		**a** Travel		
11 Depletion		**b** Total meals and entertainment .		
12 Depreciation and section 179 deduction from Form 4562 (not included in Part III)		**c** Enter 20% of line 26b subject to limitations (see Instructions) . .		
13 Dues and publications		**d** Subtract line 26c from 26b . . .		
14 Employee benefit programs		**27** Utilities and telephone		
15 Freight (not included in Part III) . . .		**28a** Wages		
16 Insurance		**b** Jobs credit		
17 Interest:		**c** Subtract line 28b from 28a . . .		
a Mortgage (paid to financial institutions)		**29** Other expenses (list type and amount):		
b Other		....		
18 Laundry and cleaning		....		
19 Legal and professional services . .		....		
20 Office expense		....		
21 Pension and profit-sharing plans . .		....		
22 Rent on business property . . .				

30 Add amounts in columns for lines 6 through 29. These are the **total deductions** . . . . ▶	**30**	
31 **Net profit or (loss).** Subtract line 30 from line 5. If a profit, enter here and on Form 1040, line 13, and on Schedule SE, line 2 (or line 5 of Form 1041 or Form 1041S). If a loss, you **MUST** go on to line 32	**31**	

32 If you have a loss, you **MUST** answer this question: "Do you have amounts for which you are not at risk in this business?" (See Instructions.) ☐ Yes ☐ No
    If "Yes," you **MUST** attach **Form 6198**. If "No," enter the loss on Form 1040, line 13, and on Schedule SE, line 2 (or line 5 of Form 1041 or Form 1041S).

For Paperwork Reduction Act Notice, see Form 1040 Instructions.   Schedule C (Form 1040)

Figure 10. Form 1040, Schedule C

The first year the couple was in business, they experienced a loss of approximately $1,500. (To get started they needed to purchase some specialized bicycling equipment and do quite a lot of advertising. They also had travel expenses connected with determining the most suitable locales for bicycle tours.) Bill and Barbara's taxable income from their pension plans and other sources that year was $18,000, but because of their business loss, they paid taxes on only $16,500.

Owing to this feature of the tax laws, people sometimes report that they are operating a money-losing business when, in fact, they are making no attempt to generate earnings from the activity. To qualify as a business, you must really be trying to make money (or at least not lose any). Avoiding trouble with the I.R.S. on this score generally requires that you show a profit at least three years out of every five.

Self-Employment Tax

When you work for someone else, you contribute to the social security system through payroll deductions. When you work for yourself, you must also make contributions. That is what self-employment tax is all about. Even if you are receiving social security benefits, you must continue to pay into the system so long as you have earnings.

Now, in 1988, self-employment tax is effectively 13.02%. This may seem high, but remember, you are making contributions as both "employer" and "employee." Furthermore, like federal income tax, self-employment tax is based on net profit, after subtracting all tax-deductible business expenses.

Schedule SE is the form used to report your earnings for the purpose of self-employment tax. You must file Schedule SE only if your net profit is $400 or more.

Estimated Tax Payments

If, like most retirees, your income is not subject to withholding, and if you expect that your total federal taxes (income tax and self-employment tax) will be $500 or more, you are required to make quarterly payments in advance. This is equivalent to having taxes withheld from your paycheck when you work for someone else.

Of course, you won't know until the end of the year just what your net profit will be, so you have to guess how much you will owe and then pay one-quarter of that amount every three months. The due dates are April 15, June 15, September 15, and January 15. Then, when you file your tax return the following April, you calculate what you actually owe. If you have paid too little in estimated taxes, you will need to make up the difference; if too much, you will receive a refund.

The I.R.S. may penalize you if your guesswork results in a substantial underpayment, however, so be careful! Rules governing penalties and ways of avoiding them are explained in a free I.R.S. pamphlet, "Tax Withholding and Estimated Tax" (Publication #505). You may also wish to consult an experienced mini-businessperson about how he or she handles "quarterlies," or perhaps get the advice of a tax specialist.

Form 1040-ES is used to make quarterly estimated tax payments.

Federal Identification Number

In completing your federal tax returns, you must identify your business by a number. If you are sole proprietor (see Chapter 9) and have no employees, your social security number is all that is required. A partnership or corporation, or any business with employees, needs a "Federal Employer Identification Number." Apply to the I.R.S. using Form SS-4. There is no fee. (A partnership that does not plan to hire employees should indicate this on the form. Otherwise, the I.R.S. will send, and expect you to complete, payroll tax forms.)

State and Local Taxes

Most states tax individual incomes, and their rules for calculating business expenses are either identical or quite similar to those of the federal government. Some states also tax businesses, usually on the basis of total sales (rather than net profit). Your state may also have a business property and/or inventory tax. Check also to see whether you will need to apply for a state identification number.

In addition to the taxes that you owe on your own behalf, you may be required to collect taxes from your customers and pass them on to state or local government agencies. Sales tax is the most common of these (see Chapter 9), but there may be others in your state or city. For example, if you take paying guests into your home, as a bed-and-breakfast inn, you may have to collect a "short-term occupancy" tax. Your state and local tax offices can supply you with details.

A Final Note

Tax laws change from year to year, sometimes in important ways. Before taking any action based upon your reading of this chapter, be sure to check with a knowledgeable source to make sure that the information is still accurate.

For More Information

SMALL TIME OPERATOR: HOW TO START YOUR OWN SMALL BUSINESS, KEEP YOUR BOOKS, PAY YOUR TAXES AND STAY OUT OF TROUBLE, by Bernard Kamoroff. Bell Springs Publishing, Laytonville, CA, revised every year.
Easy to understand and fun to read, this book is a highly recommended guide to small business taxation.

TAX GUIDE FOR SMALL BUSINESS, Publication #334, U.S. Internal Revenue Service, revised every year.

A comprehensive coverage of all aspects of income tax reporting, more perhaps than you want to know. To request a free copy, call your local office of the I.R.S. (look under U.S. Government in the telephone book). The I.R.S. also publishes pamphlets on specific tax subjects. Some you may wish to have are: "Business Expenses" (#535), "Information for Business Taxpayers" (#583), "Business Use of Your Home" (#587), and Business Use of a Car" (#917). These too are available for the asking.

TAX SAVER: HOME OFFICE, by Jay Knepp, CPA. Sunset Books, Menlo Park, CA, 1987.

A detailed guide for home office tax deductions, along with forms for maintaining necessary records.

Chapter 9
Making It Legal

Many mini-businesses begin very informally, and sometimes even unintentionally. This happened to Lloyd, a retired dentist, who made silver jewelry as a hobby. He had always given his creations as gifts, but for fun decided to try selling a few items at a fair sponsored by the senior center. The proprietor of a nearby crafts shop was in attendance and purchased a number of Lloyd's pieces to add to the store's inventory. Buoyed by this expression of interest in his work, Lloyd participated in several other craft fairs and also left some items for sale on consignment at another store in town.

Soon Lloyd was earning an average of $300 a month above his expenses, without ever thinking of himself as being "in business." He was grateful when his wife casually inquired whether he had been collecting sales tax on the items he sold at the fairs. It had never occurred to him to investigate whether this might be necessary. He realized that the time had come to acknowledge that he was indeed operating a mini-business, and to look into the rules and regulations governing his activities.

Lloyd's situation is quite typical. He operated "illegally" for a time, but he did so inadvertently and without getting into trouble. Some mini-businesspeople continue in this mode for years. On the other hand, there have been occasional cases where mini-businesses have been heavily fined for failure to comply with particular laws.

Although it is by no means necessary to start out by checking into every possible regulation that might apply to your business activity, it is a good idea to gradually familiarize yourself with pertinent city, county, state and federal laws and requirements. This chapter will introduce you to some of the more common ones. To learn more, consult the references listed at the end of the chapter.

Licenses and Permits

Business License. Most towns and cities have some sort of business license, and sometimes counties and states do too. Requirements and fees vary widely from one community to the next. In some places home-based businesses do not need a license, in others the fee is low, and in still others you will be charged according to the dollar volume of your business. You can find out more by contacting your city's tax department or your city (or county) clerk's office.

Specialized Permits. Certain types of businesses need to gain approval from specific local or state government departments. For example, if your mini-business involves food, you will probably need a permit from the county health department. Child care in your home and door-to-door sales are other businesses that typically require special permits. Your county clerk and state department of consumer affairs can supply more information.

Business Name Registration. If you have decided to use a special business name, such as Strawflower Stoneware (rather than Mary Smith's Stoneware), you should file a "fictitious business name statement." In most states, such a statement is legally required if your business name does not include the surnames of all the owners, or if it implies that there are owners other than the ones identified by name.

Thus, both Mary's Stoneware and Mary Smith & Associates would need to be registered, since the former does not incorporate Mary's surname and the use of the word "associates" in the latter implies that there are additional owners. The rationale for this requirement is that it serves to let the community know who really owns the businesses operating there.

Just another piece of legal red tape? In some ways, yes, but registering your business name is good for you too. Once registered, the name is yours; no one else in the county can use it, and perhaps more importantly, no one can prevent you from using it. For example, Mary might operate under the name Strawflower Stoneware for years, but if she did not register the name, another business could not only begin using it, but could also force Mary to give it up.

The county clerk's office is the place to register your business name. A small fee is usually required. Then you need to publish an announcement of your "fictitious business name" in a local newspaper. This will be printed along with the other legal notices, probably just before or just after the classified ads. The notice must appear once a week for four weeks. The county clerk can help you figure out how to get your notice published efficiently and cheaply.

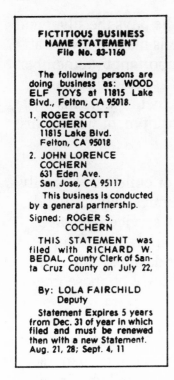

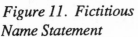

*Figure 11. Fictitious
Name Statement*

Figure 12. Seller's Permit

Figure 11 shows a "fictitious name statement" published in a California newspaper. It was filed by two brothers who had begun an at-home mini-business that involved manufacturing wooden toys. Note that only one home can be listed as the firm's business address. This is where all official mail will be sent.

A "fictitious business name" is sometimes called a "D.B.A." This stands for "doing business as." A careful reading of the first paragraph of Figure 11 will reveal how this term originated.

Seller's Permit. If your state, like most, has a sales tax, and if you sell a product directly to the consumer (rather than to a shop), you are required to collect the necessary tax and transmit it to your state tax office. On the positive side, this makes you exempt from paying sales tax when you purchase materials or products that will eventually be resold to the consumer.

Consequently, Lloyd need not pay sales tax when he buys the silver and other materials he uses to make jewelry, but when he sells his handiwork at fairs, he should collect tax from his customers. It is important to remember that your sales tax exemption applies only to items that are resold as part of your business activity. When Lloyd bought a filing cabinet to store his financial records, he paid sales tax, since this piece of equipment was for his own use rather than for resale.

Purely service businesses (such as housecleaning or child care) usually need not worry about collecting sales tax, but if any product changes hands, watch out! You may believe that you are charging for a service you have performed, but the law may define the situation differently. For example, graphic artists must sometimes charge sales tax on their designs, depending on the form in which the work is delivered. You can get advice on these gray areas from your state tax department.

If you determine that your business activity is subject to sales tax, or if you want to avoid paying sales tax when buying materials used to manufacture your product, you will need to obtain a seller's permit (also called a "resale number"). There is no fee, but if you expect to do a great deal of business in your first year, you may be asked to leave a deposit. Consult your state tax office for the name and location of the agency responsible for issuing seller's permits. An example of a seller's permit is shown in Figure 12 on the previous page.

Having a seller's permit is not directly related to whether you will be eligible to buy products or materials at "wholesale" prices. Each supplier sets his or her own policies and pricing schedule. In some cases you will be asked to supply your resale number; in others, a verbal statement that the products are for resale will be sufficient.

Occupational Licenses. All states license certain types of occupations. Just as doctors cannot practice their profession without a license, neither can (in most states) plumbers, marriage counselors, truckers, real estate agents, and many others. These regulations are designed to protect the public.

If you plan to pursue a mini-business that requires an occupational license, you are probably already aware of the need for a license and the procedures for obtaining one. Only rarely are mini-businesses surprised to find themselves in trouble on this score. Vince is a case in point.

Since Vince owned a small panel truck, he was often asked to help his neighbors with moving and hauling jobs. They usually paid him a little to compensate him for the gas and his trouble. Vince realized that there was a strong demand for this type of service, and that helping people move could be a satisfying mini-business.

A classified ad in the newspaper brought Vince several customers, as well as a call from the state Public Utilities Commission informing him that he must either apply for a mover's license or cease advertising to the general public. Vince decided that the amount of extra money he might earn was not worth the trouble and expense of applying for a license, and he returned to his former practice of working only for people he knew or who were referred to him by people he knew. He didn't earn quite as much this way, but felt this was the best solution for a "small time operator" like himself.

Others in Vince's circumstances have decided differently. If you think your mini-business requires an occupational license, you might want to talk with people doing similar work about their experiences in this area.

To learn more about occupational licenses, contact your state department of consumer affairs.

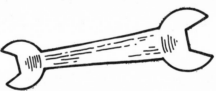

Federal Regulations. Only a few types of businesses require federal *licenses*, and these are seldom of the small-scale, at-home variety discussed in this book. Radio stations, interstate bus lines, drug manufacturers and investment counselors are among the businesses needing federal licenses.

There are, however, federal *regulations* that pertain to the operation of the smallest businesses. For example, mail order businesses are required to ship merchandise within a specified period of time, and manufacturers of clothing must label their products as to composition and recommended care. Other federal laws concern truth-in-packaging and the nature of guarantees. The Federal Trade Commission can provide you with more details. Look under U.S. Government in your telephone book, or write to the F.T.C., Washington, D.C., 20580.

Legal Structures

Businesses may be sole proprietorships, partnerships or corporations. These terms refer to the type of ownership arrangement and the resulting legal responsibilities of the owner(s). The legal structure of a business may not correspond exactly to the way things are done on a day-to-day basis, but it is important to understand the responsibilities that go with each type of structure to avoid trouble and confusion.

Sole Proprietorship. This is a business that is owned by one person or, in community property states, by a husband and wife. There may be employees or co-workers, but one person (or couple) is financially responsible for the affairs of the business. If you are already operating a mini-business and haven't taken the steps necessary to form a partnership or a corporation, you are a sole proprietor. It's as simple as that.

Sole proprietors are not legally separate from the business they are operating. This means several things. One of these has already been discussed in the chapter on taxes; sole proprietors file only their own personal tax returns (with Schedule C as an attachment). They do not need a federal identification number (so long as they don't have employees), and they don't have to file a separate tax return for their business. Red tape is minimized for the sole proprietor.

Because there is no legal separation between the owner and his or her business, sole proprietors must be prepared to be personally responsible for any financial obligations that the business develops. For example, if you borrow money to start your mini-business or purchase materials on credit or are sued by a customer, you must pay these bills even if you have to take the money from your personal savings account or, worse still, sell some of your personal possessions. There is no use arguing that these are business and not personal debts; you *are* the business.

Of course, you won't have problems if you are cautious in your expenditures and are adequately insured, but it is important to understand your liability in these matters.

The sole proprietorship is far and away the most common form of business structure.

Partnership. A partnership is like a sole proprietorship that is owned by more than one person. Just as the sole proprietor is legally inseparable from his or her business, so are partners. Like sole proprietors, partners pay personal income taxes on the business' profits (these may be divided up in a variety of ways) and are personally responsible for business debts.

With partnerships, however, this responsibility extends to debts incurred by any of the partners. If your partner, while representing the business, borrows money, purchases materials on credit, or injures someone, you are equally responsible for covering these costs. If your partner has no money in the bank and you do, you may end up having to pay the whole thing. (This may apply if you are carrying out some sort of business activity with another person, even if you don't think of yourselves as "partners." Be extra cautious in such circumstances.)

Paying taxes is slightly more complicated for partnerships than for sole proprietorships. Partnerships must have a federal identification number and file a partnership tax return. This, in turn, necessitates a bit more record-keeping.

These legal responsibilities often seem trivial when balanced against the advantages of working with one or more partners. Further, a partnership agreement can help to avoid many potential problems. These issues are discussed in more detail in Chapter 10.

Corporation. Corporations are owned by stockholders, who collect part of the business' profits, depending on the number of shares they own. Unlike sole proprietorships and partnerships, corporations are separate legal entities, independent of the individuals who own them. This limits, to some degree, stockholders' liability for business debts.

Corporations can be costly and complicated to establish, are heavily regulated, and sometimes pay more taxes. Some large organizations find incorporation advantageous, but the mini-business that would benefit from becoming a corporation is rare indeed. Even if you hope to eventually grow out of the mini-business category, you need not begin as a corporation. It is quite easy to change from one type of legal structure to another, so postpone taking this step until you are *very* sure it will be to your benefit.

Non-Profit Corporation. A special form of the corporation, the non-profit structure, is designed for organizations which provide social, educational or religious services to the community. Examples include groups offering home care for the frail elderly or operating informational centers on the benefits of solar energy. Non-profit organizations do not have stockholders or any other "owners;" they are governed by boards of directors whose members serve as volunteers.

A non-profit organization may charge for its services and, like any other business, must take in more money than it spends if it is to survive. However, an excess of income over expenses is considered a "surplus" rather than a "profit," and is retained by the organization. A surplus may be saved for a rainy day, used to improve services, or applied to the purchase of new equipment. It may not be used to enrich the members of the board of directors.

If you expect to earn any money from the work you do in a non-profit organization, you must be hired as an employee by the board of directors. This involves the organization in all of the paperwork required of any business that takes on employees (see Chapter 10).

Non-profit corporations can apply to the I.R.S. for tax-exempt status. If granted, the organization does not pay federal taxes and, in addition, may be eligible to receive tax-deductible gifts from individuals and businesses. If you think your mini-business qualifies as a non-profit organization, and if you have realistic hopes of raising money by asking people for donations, then it may be worthwhile investigating the non-profit form of organization.

The application procedures for non-profit incorporation are fairly complicated, but not too costly. An attorney or accountant (ideally one who will volunteer his or her time to your good cause) is essential.

To learn more, consult the book *Starting and Running a Non-Profit Organization* listed at the end of this chapter.

Insurance

You may not need any insurance beyond that which you already have for your home, car and so on. Just to be sure, it is a good idea to check with your insurance agent or broker. Here are some questions to consider:

If you have customers or clients coming to your home, will your homeowner's or renter's insurance protect you if they are injured while on your property? Perhaps you will need to pay a small fee in order to have a rider added to your general liability policy. Similarly, will your homeowner's or renter's policy cover your business equipment and materials against loss from fire, theft and vandalism? If your business-related possessions represent a significant amount of money, you may need a rider or even a separate policy.

Automobile or truck insurance is of two types--liability and damage. Again, make certain that your existing policy will cover any vehicle while it is being used for business. This is particularly important with regard to liability insurance which protects you in the event someone is injured by the vehicle.

Workers' compensation insurance is a must if you have employees. It covers employee injuries and loss of pay resulting from accidents on the job. "Workers' comp" is mandatory in many states (with premiums fixed by state law) but important to carry even if not legally required. Otherwise, you might find yourself paying employee medical expenses out of your own pocket.

Do you need any other types of special business insurance? For example, is there is any chance that a product you sell could harm the user--such as a face cream that could cause a rash? If so, you may need to carry product liability insurance. Similarly, some service businesses will want to consider service liability insurance. Your agent or broker will be able to advise you.

Summary

This chapter has provided an overview of the most frequently encountered legal requirements involved in establishing a mini-business, and **Exercise 13** offers a way for you to summarize what you have learned. Which requirements apply to your proposed mini-business? Where can you go for more information?

As your business gets underway, you will probably encounter a variety of other situations involving the law. You may want to copyright a jingle you have written, have problems with faulty materials, or be asked to sign a contract. Books, government agencies, or more experienced businesspeople may be able to give you the necessary information about these matters.

If, however, you still have questions about local, state or federal laws that have not been answered to your satisfaction, a lawyer or accountant (if the issue concerns taxes) should be consulted. If you do not have a family attorney, your local Lawyer Referral Service can make an appointment for you with a specialist in small business law. A half-hour consultation is available for a very nominal fee.

A Final Note

It is often said that small businesses are over-regulated, and this point of view has some validity. At the same time, it is important to remember that most laws were made to protect consumers, the general public and/or the businessperson him- or herself. If all businesses were honest, careful, concerned with preserving the environment and oriented toward serving their local communities, the need for government regulation would be much reduced. Such, unfortunately, is not the case. The result is what often seems like an overwhelming mountain of red tape, especially for the beginning mini-businessperson.

Rather than becoming upset or worried, however, the best response is to think of the legal thicket as new territory to be explored. Have you ever lived in another country or moved into a different job situation? If so, you will recall all the new rules--written and unwritten--that you needed to learn. You probably felt quite uncomfortable at first, but gradually figured out what needed to be done and how others would react if you made a mistake.

It is the same in starting a business. As you deal with government agencies you will quickly learn how to cope. You will figure out who to talk to, what questions to ask, and how (or whether) to fill out forms. Soon it will all be second nature, and you will wonder why you ever felt confused.

For More Information

SMALL TIME OPERATOR: HOW TO START YOUR OWN SMALL BUSINESS, KEEP YOUR BOOKS, PAY YOUR TAXES AND STAY OUT OF TROUBLE, by Bernard Kamoroff. Bell Springs Publishing, Laytonville, CA, revised every year.
> *This book, also listed in Chapters 7 and 8, offers an excellent summary of the steps needed to "stay out of trouble."*

THE LAW (IN PLAIN ENGLISH) FOR SMALL BUSINESS, by Leonard D. DuBoff. Madrona Publishing, Seattle, WA, 1987.
> *Straightforward, sensible coverage of a wide range of legal topics, including insurance, leases, employees, contracts, consumer protection, and consignment selling.*

MAKING IT LEGAL: A LAW PRIMER FOR THE CRAFTMAKER, VISUAL ARTIST AND WRITER, by Marion Davidson and Martha Blue. McGraw-Hill, New York, NY, 1979.
> *Despite outdated material on taxation, the extensive treatment of contracts and copyright makes this an enduringly valuable reference.*

STARTING AND RUNNING A NON-PROFIT ORGANIZATION, by Joan Hummel. University of Minnesota Press, Minneapolis, MN, 1980.
> *Covering far more than the legal angle, this is an excellent resource on all aspects of operating an effective organization.*

Chapter 10
Working With Others

Throughout this book there have been allusions to the value of cooperation in the world of small business. This includes cooperative relationships among businesses, such as referring customers to one another, sharing in the purchase of equipment or joining together to save money on advertising. Even better, for many people, is teaming up with others to start and operate a mini-business together.

Partnerships

Partnerships offer many advantages. In business decision-making, two (or more) heads may be better than one. Partners can prevent one another from making foolish mistakes, and when several people pool their experiences and perspectives, they often see solutions that a single individual overlooks.

Partners can pool money too, and this may make possible a mini-business that could not otherwise get off the ground. Equipment or materials that would be too costly for one person to purchase may be well within the reach of two or three partners.

Similarly, partnerships can combine skills, abilities and community contacts in such a way that the business is much stronger than one run by a sole proprietor. For example, an excellent craftsperson who has no talent for selling or bookkeeping may pair up with someone who has a natural bent for the "business end" of things. The members of a group starting a job placement service for seniors will know people from a wide range of industries and agencies.

Time flexibility is often easier to come by in a partnership business. If one partner experiences temporary health problems or wants to take a vacation or to spend time with children visiting from out-of-town, the business need not be shut down. The remaining partner(s) can carry on. (Of course, time off needs to be fairly distributed and mutually agreed upon.)

Finally, partnerships can be fun. Particularly in the early months of operating a mini-business, when there is a great deal of both uncertainty and excitement, it is satisfying to be able to share these feelings with others who are experiencing them too. People who might otherwise be reluctant to visit a government office or ask questions of the proprietor of an existing business find their self-confidence bolstered when in the company of a partner.

The friendly social contact provided by one or more partners is also a big plus. Although isolation can be a problem for home-based businesspeople of all ages, it is particularly important for retired men and women to avoid this mental health hazard. A partnership business is one way of making your life more stimulating and enjoyable.

On the other hand, partnerships can be stressful. Partners may find that they have different ideas about the conduct of their joint business activities. Or one person may feel that the other is not working hard enough (or is a workaholic who doesn't know how to have fun), is too disorganized (or too fussy), is overly bossy (or lacks initiative). How can problems such as these be avoided?

A partnership is in some ways like a marriage. Like a good marriage, a good partnership begins with compatibility and lasts because of good communication.

Before entering a partnership, take a good look at yourself and at your potential partner(s). Begin by asking yourself whether you are really the "partner type." Are you tolerant of other people's quirks and shortcomings? Can you compromise? Are you willing to discuss things before taking action? Are you able to let others know, in a constructive way, when they are doing things that make you unhappy? Can you accept constructive criticism from others? "Yes" answers to these questions bode well for your success in a partner relationship.

Next, take some time to figure out whether you and your partner(s) will work well together as a team. Here are some of the things to be considered:

(1) Are you personally compatible? Do you enjoy each other's company? Do you find it easy to communicate with each other?

(2) What are each person's work habits? Have you ever worked together on a project, for example, in an organization you both belong to? Were you satisfied with your compatibility in such matters as how well-organized, careful, creative or energetic each person was? Were you satisfied with the way you divided up the work? (If you have never worked together before, sit down and discuss these issues.)

(3) Do the partners have compatible reasons for wanting to start a mini-business and similar ideas about how it should be conducted? If one person is interested primarily in having a good time and meeting new people, while the other wants to earn as much money as possible, they will likely find themselves in frequent disagreement about how to carry out their business.

Even more basically, are you certain that you and your partner(s) have the same conception of the kind of business you will start? A "gardening business," for example, may mean different things to different people. To test your similarity in this regard, it might be helpful for each partner to complete Exercise 6 ("Defining My Business Idea") independently, and then compare notes.

(4) Have you talked over the various responsibilities involved in running a mini-business--manufacturing the product or performing the service, advertising and publicity, financial record-keeping, and so on--and decided on a way of dividing these up that is comfortable for each person? Do you know how many hours per week each person plans to work on the business?

(5) What about business finances? How will you divide up the starting costs? What equipment and materials will each person contribute? If there is a financial loss during the early months, will this be absorbed equally by each partner or in some other way? How will profits be divided? Do these arrangements seem fair to everyone concerned?

If all partners are satisfied with the answers to these questions, your business relationship will be off to a good start. You will also have begun a process of open communication that you should strive to continue as time goes on. If things don't seem to be working out the way you had expected--whether because one person appears to be working harder than the others, getting his or her way too often, or whatever--you need to be able to discuss the situation and find a solution. Letting problems build up is a sure way to send your partnership to the "divorce court."

It is also a good idea to get your initial expectations down on paper in the form of a partnership agreement. A written agreement is not legally necessary, but is strongly recommended as a way of avoiding possible misunderstandings. If you decide to do things differently in the future, it can always be changed. *The Partnership Book*, listed at the end of this chapter, gives complete directions for writing a partnership agreement.

A Family Business?

Starting a mini-business together with family members--a spouse, brother or sister, grown children--is quite common among retirees. There are good reasons for this. In many cases, relatives are the people we know best and trust most. Similar backgrounds and years of close association give family members a lot in common; they know what to expect of each other and they feel at ease in each other's company.

A business with relatives is like any other partnership, only more so. As with any partnership, it is important to make sure you are compatible as business partners and that your goals and expectations are similar. Indeed, it is probably more important because if you end up quarreling, the consequences will be even more unfortunate. A written partnership agreement is just as desirable among family members as in any other kind of business partnership.

The things that cause problems in a business relationship are sometimes different when the partners are close relatives. This is because personal issues may carry over. For example, a parent may be unwilling to allow a grown child to function as a truly equal partner, or a husband may expect his wife to take on a support role while he makes all the important decisions. And, owing to the close emotional ties between the partners, their feelings about these problems may be more intense.

At the same time, the motivation to iron things out is greater when your partner is someone you really care about. This does not mean one partner giving in or trying to act as if problems did not exist. Rather, it requires taking the time to find a mutually satisfying solution. When this happens, the personal relationship will be strengthened by the pleasure of shared accomplishment, and the business will be a stronger one too.

Cooperatives

Throughout the United States and Europe are numerous consumer cooperatives, such as grocery stores that are owned by the shoppers. This is what most people think of when they hear the word "co-op." But businesses can be owned and managed by the people who work there, and these are co-ops too. Worker co-ops range from large organizations, such as International Group Plans, a 300 person insurance company, to mini-businesses of two or three people.

What is the difference between a small worker co-op and a business partnership? There need not be any difference at all. A partnership is a particular kind of legal structure, one of several that a co-op may choose to use. A cooperative is any organization that is owned and democratically controlled by its members, and this can be true of small business partnerships.

So, if there are several of you who own and manage a mini-business together, you may wish to think of yourselves as a co-op. (In some states you cannot use the word "co-op" in your business name unless you incorporate under laws that govern cooperative corporations. This only limits your choice of name. It doesn't mean you must refrain from telling your customers that you are a cooperatively owned and managed business.)

Mini-businesspeople who choose this option have generally been active in the cooperative movement. By calling their business a co-op, they reinforce their own commitment to cooperative principles and they help educate others about the value of democratic control of economic institutions.

A third type of cooperative exists when people who individually produce products join together to sell what they have made. These are known as producer co-ops and are commonly found among artists and craftspeople, although any type of product can be sold in this way. Co-ops of this sort are not only effective sales outlets, but also help to alleviate the loneliness that home-based artists and craftspeople sometimes experience.

To learn more about cooperatives, consult the book *We Own It*, which is listed at the end of the chapter.

Employees

There may come a time when you need to hire someone to help you with your mini-business. There is too much work for you to accomplish by yourself, or there are tasks you are not able or don't want to do. People who work for you fall into two categories--independent contractors and employees.

Independent contractors are self-employed businesspeople, just like yourself. They set their own prices (although negotiation is sometimes possible), supply their own equipment, and arrange to do the work when it is mutually convenient. They usually have several customers or clients. Examples of independent contractors that might be hired by a mini-business are bookkeepers, delivery people, and office cleaners.

Jake and Bertie's situation is a case in point. Jake's mini-business is selling cookbooks by mail order. When first starting out, he kept all his own financial records but found this part of being in business very tedious and time-consuming. As soon as he could afford it, he hired a bookkeeper to take over this responsibility.

Bertie, another retiree, comes once a week to pay Jake's bills, record income and expenses, and fill out any necessary tax forms. Jake learned about Bertie from a small ad she had placed in the senior center newsletter: "Bookkeeping for small businesses, $8 per hour," and he hired her after checking with several of her other clients to make sure they were satisfied with her services.

When Bertie takes care of Jake's paperwork, she brings her own calculator and works at the kitchen table, while Jake responds to mail order requests in his garage workroom. If she doesn't have time to stay, she picks up the bills, checkbook and ledgers and takes these home with her, delivering the completed work to Jake the next day. At the end of each month, she draws up a profit-and-loss statement and sends Jake an invoice indicating how much he owes her. Bertie is an independent contractor, and Jake's life has been greatly simplified by engaging her services.

At one point, Jake also considered taking on an employee. His mail order business was doing fairly well and he knew that, with a little more advertising, he could expand significantly. Then he would have to hire someone to help him package and mail the cookbooks. An assistant would be an employee rather than an independent contractor, because Jake would be that person's boss, telling him or her what needed to be done and how to do it.

However, when Jake looked into the requirements for becoming an employer, he decided against taking this step. He felt that the paperwork was excessive and that he'd be better off keeping his business small and manageable. Here's what Jake learned:

(1) Employers must withhold federal and state income taxes from their employee's paycheck, and must also deduct social security payments. These must be deposited in an authorized bank and reported on special tax forms.

(2) Employers must also contribute to the employee's social security account. This is deposited in the authorized bank along with the withheld taxes. (Note that this contribution is entirely separate from self-employment tax, discussed in Chapter 8. Self-employment tax is credited to your own social security account. The payments referred to here are those you, as an employer, make on behalf of your employee.)

(3) Employers must pay into both federal and state unemployment insurance programs. Special forms are required for each.

(4) Employers must carry Workers' Compensation Insurance.

(5) Employers are required to keep a separate and detailed payroll ledger and to prepare year-end earnings statements (W-2 forms) for their employees.

(6) Employers must familiarize themselves with a variety of regulations affecting their treatment of employees, including minimum wage laws and health and safety standards.

All this was more red tape than Jake wanted to contemplate, but you may decide that having one or more employees is the right thing for you. You may look upon the paperwork as a challenge, and a small price to pay for the assistance and company that an employee can provide. If so, you should consult the reference works listed at the end of the chapter for more information.

In taking this step, you will also want to think about ways of making the employer-employee arrangement a mutually satisfying one. Like a partnership, this "working together" relationship deserves to be carefully nurtured. What will motivate your employee to do a good job? How can you help him or her to develop new skills and learn more about the business world? How can you encourage him or her to raise problems and offer suggestions? What are the most constructive ways of providing him or her with helpful feedback? How can you have fun together and still get the work done? In short, what will help you grow in mutual respect and build your effectiveness as a team? As with a partnership, this is what "working together" is all about.

For More Information

THE PARTNERSHIP BOOK, Third Edition, by Denis Clifford and Ralph Warner. Nolo Press, Berkeley, CA, 1987.
> *Detailed directions for writing a partnership agreement and thinking about the partnership relationship. An excellent resource, clearly written and fun to read.*

TAX INFORMATION ON PARTNERSHIPS, Publication #541, U.S. Internal Revenue Service, revised every year.
> *Explains how to file a partnership tax return.*

HOW TO START A FAMILY BUSINESS AND MAKE IT WORK, by Jerome Goldstein. M. Evans & Co., New York, NY, 1984.
> *A practical guide for those who are considering going into business with family members. Discusses both the pros and cons of such an endeavor.*

WE OWN IT: STARTING AND MANAGING COOPS, COLLECTIVES AND EMPLOYEE-OWNED VENTURES, by Peter Jan Honigsberg, Bernard Kamoroff and Jim Beatty. Bell Springs Publishing, Laytonville, CA, 1982.

Describes the legal, financial and managerial procedures involved in setting up and running all kinds of cooperatives. Clear and complete, with numerous interesting examples.

MESSAGES, by Matthew McKay, Martha Davis and Patrick Fanning. New Harbinger Publications, Oakland, CA, 1983.

Ways to improve communication, give and receive constructive criticism, negotiate, and deal with conflict. Good for personal as well as business relationships!

"Personnel Guidelines," SMALL BUSINESS REPORTER (SBR-115)

A good, brief overview of all the facets of being an employer, both legal and managerial. Available at Bank of America branches in California, or write to the Bank of America, Department 3120, P.O. Box 37000, San Francisco, CA, 94137, for mail order information.

CIRCULAR E: EMPLOYER'S TAX GUIDE, Publication #15, U.S. Internal Revenue Service, revised every year.

This document explains all of the rules about payroll taxes, withholding, social security contributions, and related matters.

Chapter 11
Summing Up

If you have read this far, it probably means that the idea of starting a mini-business intrigues you. You've seen that this can be a vehicle for expressing your creativity, learning new skills, meeting people, and serving your community, as well as earning extra money. And you've learned the steps involved in establishing and operating your own small-scale, home-based business.

But perhaps you still feel hesitant, wondering if you have enough information or unsure just how to go about actualizing your plans. The aim of this concluding chapter is to answer these concerns so that you can "get down to business."

Where to Get Help

Each individual's circumstances are different, mini-businesses are different, and communities are different. It is therefore unlikely that this small book has answered every one of your questions about starting and running a mini-business. It has provided you with all the basics, but there is probably more that you would like to know. Where can you turn for assistance?

One of the best resources is *other mini-businesspeople*, especially those who are doing work similar to your own. If you want to operate a blood pressure clinic at senior centers, it would be best to talk with other individuals and groups who provide health care services. But even if your mini-business acquaintances are doing something quite different from the sort of thing you have in mind, they will still have helpful information and advice. You will probably enjoy hearing their stories too.

At the present time, the U.S. *Small Business Administration* has offices in over 100 cities nationwide. In addition to the low-cost literature described elsewhere in this book, the S.B.A. has many other services for people who want to start businesses. The most important of these is a free counseling service operated by the Service Corps of Retired Executives.

You will need to have a specific area of concern to benefit from S.C.O.R.E. counseling, such as pricing your product or deciding how to advertise. Further, the volunteer S.C.O.R.E. counselors have usually gained their experience in larger businesses, so you should make it clear that your ambitions are limited to running a successful *mini*-business. If you follow these guidelines, S.C.O.R.E. counseling can be very helpful. S.C.O.R.E. chapters organize classes for prospective business owners too. Ask about these when you telephone (look in the telephone book under U.S. Government).

The U.S. *Internal Revenue Service*, as has already been noted, supplies a wide range of free pamphlets explaining all aspects of small business taxation. In addition, you can telephone your nearest office with questions, and ask for assistance in keeping good tax records and completing required forms. The staff there will not take any initiative in helping you look for ways to save money on your taxes, however. For this you will need to consult an independent tax specialist.

The goal of the *National Alliance of Homebased Businesswomen* is to develop links among women who operate businesses from their homes, providing them with a support network and information exchange. There are local chapters in many communities. Write to the N.A.H.B., P.O. Box 306, Midland Park, NJ, 07432, for more information.

If there is a *senior employment service* in your area, its staff members may be able to offer assistance in establishing and publicizing your mini-business, or in referring you to other sources of help. Other non-profit employment centers may also be useful. Many of these offer classes, counseling and library resources for people interested in starting a business. Such services may be provided through the Y.W.C.A., a women's career center, or similar agency.

Adult education programs at your local high school or community college will probably include classes on bookkeeping and other small business topics. These are usually quite inexpensive.

As discussed in Chapter 3, most small businesses are affiliated with some sort of *trade association* which provides publications and other aids to learning about the field. Regional associations also offer the opportunity to meet and learn from others who are doing work similar to yours. Your *public library* will have a listing of trade associations and various other reference books.

Reading materials can be of great value in providing detailed information on specific subjects, as well as general guidelines, advice, ideas and inspiration. Throughout this publication there have been lists of books, magazine articles, and pamphlets that are particularly useful for beginning mini-businesspeople. At the end of this chapter there are more. You may also wish to consult your local librarian for his or her recommendations.

One caution: Books dealing with legal matters can be extremely useful in offering general information and guidelines, but cannot substitute for advice from a competent professional who is able to judge how the law applies to your specific situation. So, if you have a legal problem, do not rely solely on reading materials for an answer. Consult a *lawyer or accountant.*

Developing a Plan of Action

You now know what starting a mini-business is all about, and you know where to go for additional information and assistance. You're enthusiastic and eager to get underway, but perhaps don't quite know where to start. None of the details seem too hard, but there are so many of them!

Here are some techniques that may be helpful in overcoming these feelings. The first step is to determine where there are gaps in the skills and knowledge you will need to operate your mini-business. **Exercise 14** provides a format for doing this.

The first section of this exercise focuses on the product or service you plan to provide. As an example, suppose you intend selling framed photographs of mountain scenery. You've chosen this because you have received many compliments on your outdoor photography, and because your market research has suggested that photographs of this kind sell better if already framed. If photography has been your long-time hobby, your knowledge of photographic techniques is probably substantial, but perhaps you've had no experience in making frames. This, then, would be a skill you must acquire before you can begin.

Examine your own mini-business idea. What do you need to know before you can begin offering your chosen product or service?

The remaining sections of the exercise provide spaces to consider the skills and knowledge needed to spread the word of your mini-business, organize your finances, and anything else required to get your business off the ground. For example, if you have decided to advertise by distributing flyers, you may need to learn a little about effective flyer design. If you plan to give talks, improving your public speaking skills may be called for. Do you need to learn how to set up a record-keeping system? develop a budget? negotiate a contract? Write it down.

Be honest with yourself in assessing your weak areas, but guard against listing too many items. Include only those things that must be learned *before* actually beginning. You need not be an expert in every subject before opening your doors. Rather, expect to learn a great deal as you go along. This is part of the challenge and the fun of operating your own mini-business.

Having written down the things you really need to learn in the first column, think about the various ways you could acquire each skill or type of knowledge. This might include reading a book on the subject, taking a class, attending a workshop or lecture, consulting an expert, volunteering in an agency or small business where you can learn the skill, or asking someone to teach you (perhaps in exchange for your teaching him or her something). What are other ways to learn the things you need to know? Use the second column to write down your plan for acquiring the skills and knowledge needed to begin your mini-business.

Now you are ready to develop a concrete plan of action. Using **Exercise 15**, list everything you need to do to get your mini-business underway. This will include the learning tasks you identified in Exercise 14, as well as a range of specific questions to be answered and details to be attended to.

Here are some examples taken from the lists of several seniors who did this exercise: apply for a business license, find out where to get yard goods at wholesale prices, get business cards printed, invite friends over to brainstorm a good business name, buy typewriter, read *Small Time Operator*, check out resources at library, attend home business class at the community college, start subscription to crafts magazine, remodel basement into workroom.

When you have listed everything you can think of, evaluate each item. Is this something you *really* need to do before starting? If so, put a check under "essential." Is it something that should be done (or begun) right away because it precedes other tasks or takes a long time to accomplish? If so, put a check under "timely."

When this is finished, you have the information needed to organize a time line. When would you like to be "in business"? *Set a specific date*. Then get a long strip of paper and mark the dates and days of the week across the top, beginning with today and ending with your target date.

Starting with the items that you have checked as both essential and timely, figure out when to do each task in order to accomplish everything by your target date. Be sure to allow extra time for possible snags and setbacks--an office that is unexpectedly closed, someone taking longer than anticipated to answer your correspondence, materials which fail to arrive when promised, and so on. A good rule is to set all of your dates one to two weeks in advance of the time you think the tasks really need to be done. If this lets you begin early, so much the better.

Now tell your family and friends about your plans. Ask for their support and encouragement. Telling others is a good way to firm up your commitment, and having their backing will help you carry on should you encounter problems.

Start right away on today's tasks. Once you get involved in carrying out your plans, your knowledge and confidence will grow dramatically. Soon your mini-business will really be underway, bringing new challenges and new opportunities to your retirement years.

Good luck!

For More Information

INVEST IN YOURSELF; A WOMAN'S GUIDE TO STARTING HER OWN
BUSINESS, by Peg Moran. Doubleday and Company, Garden City, NY,
1983.
> *If you have enjoyed completing the written exercises in* STARTING A
> MINI-BUSINESS, *you will want to own this workbook, as it is
> chock-full of exercises and examples. Both men and women will find it
> of great value in planning their mini-businesses.*

CREATIVE CASH: MAKING MONEY WITH YOUR CRAFTS,
NEEDLEWORK, DESIGNS AND KNOW-HOW, Fourth Edition, by Barbara
Brabec. Aames-Allen Publishing, Huntington Beach, CA, 1986.
> *A very readable and attractively illustrated handbook on turning creative
> hobbies into mini-business activities. It includes a comprehensive list of
> resources.*

STAY HOME AND MIND YOUR OWN BUSINESS, by Jo Frohbieter-
Mueller. Betterway Publications, White Hall, VA, 1987.
> *Written for the individual who wishes to combine family responsibilities
> with work involvement, this helpful book addresses such issues as
> relationships with spouse and children, as well as discussing all aspects of
> running a business.*

THE TEENAGE ENTREPRENEUR'S GUIDE: 50 MONEY-MAKING
BUSINESS IDEAS, by Sarah Riehm. Surrey Books, Chicago, IL, 1987.
> *Describes business ideas especially suited to the young entrepreneur--
> those which require little or no expertise, capital or transportation, and
> can be scheduled around school hours.*

EXTRA CASH FOR KIDS, by Larry Belliston and Kurt Hanks. Writer's
Digest, Cincinnati, OH, 1982.
> *Ideas, start-up strategies, pricing guidelines, and other mini-business
> advice--all geared toward the interests and abilities of young people from
> 8 years of age and up.*

THAT'S A GREAT IDEA: THE NEW PRODUCT HANDBOOK, by Tony
Hirsch and Linda Foust. Ten-Speed Press, Berkeley, CA, 1987.
> *How to evaluate, produce, develop, and sell your product idea.*

"Steps to Starting a Business," SMALL BUSINESS REPORTER (SBR-110)
Briefly covers a wide variety of issues to be considered in starting a small business. Available at Bank of America branches in California, or write to the Bank of America, Department 3120, P.O. Box 37000, San Francisco, CA, 94137, for mail order information. The SMALL BUSINESS REPORTER series includes several other booklets; ask for a complete list.

STARTING AND MANAGING A SMALL BUSINESS FROM YOUR HOME (#102), U.S. Small Business Administration, Washington, D.C.
A very reasonably priced booklet with checklists to aid in your business planning. Mail order information for this and other Business Development Booklets is available from the Superintendent of Documents, U. S.Government Printing Office, Washington, D. C., 20402. Ask for SBA-115B.

"The Business Plan for Home-Based Business" (MA2.028)
A low-cost pamphlet to aid in developing a plan for your mini-business, published by the Small Business Administration. For a complete list of pamphlets and ordering information, call your local office of the S.B.A. (look under U.S. Government in the telephone book), or write to P.O. Box 15434, Fort Worth, TX 76119. Ask for SBA-115A.

THE SMALL BUSINESS INFORMATION SOURCE BOOK, by Adrian A. Paradis. Betterway Publications, White Hall, VA, 1987.
When and how to locate the information you need on all types of business-related topics.

IN BUSINESS. Published by JG Press, Box 323, Emmaus, PA, 18049.
This is a bi-monthly magazine, filled with down-to-earth advice and case studies of successful "human-sized" enterprises. Includes a section especially for part-time businesses. Write for subscription information.

NATIONAL HOME BUSINESS REPORT. Published by Barbara Brabec Productions, P.O. Box 2137, Naperville, IL, 60566.
This quarterly publication offers advice and networking for the home-based businessperson. Write for subscription information.

Appendix
Exercises

Exercise 1

Is a Mini-Business the Right Thing for Me?

Under each question, check the answer that describes what you feel or comes closest to it. Be honest with yourself.

1. Are you a self-starter?

    _____ I do things without being prodded. Nobody has to tell me to get going.

    _____ If someone gets me started, I keep going all right.

    _____ Easy does it. I don't put myself out unless I have to.

2. How do you feel about other people?

    _____ I like people. I can get along with just about anybody.

    _____ I have plenty of friends, but I feel uncomfortable meeting new people.

    _____ Most people irritate me.

3. Can you take responsibility?

    _____ I like to take charge of things and see them through.

    _____ I'll take over if I have to, but I'd rather let someone else be responsible.

    _____ It seems there's always someone else around who likes to run things, and that's fine with me.

4. How good an organizer are you?

    _____ I like to have a plan before I start. I'm usually the one to get things organized when the group wants to do something.

    _____ I do all right unless things get too complex. Then I get confused.

    _____ I like to take things as they come and not worry about having a plan.

5. Can you make decisions?

    _____ I can make up my mind pretty rapidly if I have to. It usually turns out O.K. too.

    _____ I can if I have plenty of time.

    _____ I don't like to be the one who has to decide things.

(con't)

6. Can people trust what you say?

_____ You bet they can. I don't say things I don't mean.

_____ I try to be on the level most of the time, but sometimes I just say what's easiest.

_____ Why bother if the other person doesn't know the difference.

7. Can you stick with it?

_____ If I make up my mind to do something, I always carry through.

_____ I usually finish what I start, so long as it's going well.

_____ If it doesn't go well right from the beginning, I quit.

8. How good is your health?

_____ I am in excellent health.

_____ I have enough energy for most things I want to do.

_____ I run out of energy sooner than most of my friends seem to.

Checks beside the first answer to each question indicate good potential for business success; the second answer suggests the possible need for a partner(s) to balance weak areas; too many checks beside the third answer is a warning that you will probably not do well in the business world.

What do you conclude from this exercise? Is a mini-business the right thing for you?

Exercise 2

Business Ideas Based on the Things I Most Enjoy Doing

In this column, make a list of the things you most enjoy doing.

In this column, use the method of of brainstorming to make a list of mini-businesses based on the things you most enjoy doing.

Exercise 3

Business Ideas Based on My Special Skills and Talents

In this column, make a list of your special skills, talents and areas of expertise--the things you do especially well. Include special areas of knowledge.

In this column, use the method of brainstorming to make a list of mini-businesses based on your special skills and talents.

Exercise 4

Business Ideas Based on My Community Concerns and Causes

In this column, make a list of the community groups, problems and political causes you care about most.

In this column, use the method of brainstorming to make a list of mini-businesses based on your community concerns and causes.

Exercise 5

Business Ideas Based on _____

In this column, make a list of one of the following: (1) objects or spaces available to you that could be used as the basis of a mini-business, (2) jobs other people do--or have done--from time to time, (3) things you'd like to learn to do.	In this column, use the method of brainstorming to make a list of mini-businesses based on the items in the first column.

Exercise 6

Defining My Business Idea

1. What do you plan to offer? Exactly what product(s) or service(s) will you provide? Be as specific as possible.

2. To whom will you offer your product(s) or service(s)? What will be their ages, occupations, family situations, income levels, political attitudes, and so on? Where will they live? (If your customers will be businesses rather than individuals, what size and type of business and where will they be located?)

3. What else is an integral part of your business idea? (Location? Atmosphere? Size? Mode of organization?)

When you have written out the answers to the above questions, show this page to a friend. Ask him/her to tell you whether your idea is clearly described. Can he/she form a concrete mental image of what you will be doing as you conduct your business? Is that image the same as the one you have in mind? If not, go back and try to define your idea more clearly.

Exercise 7

Needs and Goals I Want My Business to Satisfy

People have different reasons for wanting to start a mini-business, and different needs they want their business to satisfy. In the first column, check those needs and goals that are important to you. Be sure to add any that aren't listed. Then think carefully about your proposed mini-business. Imagine what it will be like to operate your business on a daily basis. In the second column, check those needs and goals your mini-business will probably satisfy.

	Important To Me	My Business Will Satisfy
Learn new skills..	_____	_____
Have daily variety of activities....................	_____	_____
Express creativity...	_____	_____
Meet new people...	_____	_____
Exercise leadership......................................	_____	_____
Work in a group...	_____	_____
Work independently......................................	_____	_____
See my family and friends as often as possible..	_____	_____
Become better known in my community....	_____	_____
Have flexible hours on a daily basis...........	_____	_____
Be able to take time off for lengthy vacations...................................	_____	_____
Work no more than _____ hours per week..	_____	_____
Help to change the world for the better.......	_____	_____
Serve youth/the elderly/the poor/ other_____.................	_____	_____
Provide a quality product.............................	_____	_____
Provide a needed service..............................	_____	_____
Be physically active.....................................	_____	_____
Not require physical activity........................	_____	_____
Be outdoors as much as possible..................	_____	_____
Be able to stay indoors.................................	_____	_____

(con't)

	Important To Me	My Business Will Satisfy
Be busy, work under pressure...................	_____	_____
Be tranquil..	_____	_____
Other:_____	_____	_____
Other:_____	_____	_____

What do you conclude from this exercise? Is there a close correspondence between the first and second columns? If not, can you think of ways to modify your business idea so that it will better satisfy your needs and goals?

Exercise 8

Calculating Starting Costs

Which of the following do you anticipate needing to get your mini-business underway? For each, estimate how much it will cost. You can get help from the sources listed in the last column. If you don't expect to have a particular expense (you don't need the item or already have it), leave the space blank.

General   **Who Can Help Estimate**

Business license, permits
    (see Chapter 9)   _____   City, county offices
Start-up advertising--
    business cards, etc.
    (see Chapter 6)   _____   Printer, advertising media
Accounting advice
    (see Chapters 7-8)   _____   Accountant
Legal advice (see Chapter 9) _____   Lawyer Referral Service
Insurance (see Chapter 9)   _____   Insurance agent

Home Office/Workshop

Remodeling/redecorating   _____   Contractor, lumber yard
Telephone--if you have   or paint store
    a special business
    telephone installed   _____   Telephone company
Office supplies   _____   Stationery store
Equipment, furniture,
    machinery, tools   _____   Appropriate retail store,
                                                  want ads (for used items)

Product Businesses

For manufacturers, enough
    raw materials for
    initial production   _____   Wholesale suppliers
For retailers, starting
    inventory   _____   Wholesale suppliers
Sales tax deposit
    (see Chapter 9)   _____   State tax office

(con't)

Other Starting Costs
Make a list below and
enter the total here   _____

Total Starting Costs   _____

How do you feel about this total? Are you comfortable paying this amount of money to get your mini-business underway? Imagine the worst--that you lost all the money you put into starting costs. Can you afford this? If not, is there some way to cut down on these expenses (bartering, borrowing equipment, and so on) or of modifying the nature of the business to make it less costly?

Exercise 9

Determining Customer Interest

1. What product(s) or service(s) do you plan to provide? (Transfer your answer from Exercise 6).

2. Who will be your customers or clients? (Transfer your answer from Exercise 6).

3. Why will these customers be interested in what you plan to offer? What needs do they have that your business will satisfy? For example, will your product be durable, uniquely designed, low in price, tasty, efficient? Will your service be fast, careful, personalized, conveniently located?

4. Does it seem likely that your group of potential customers will be sufficiently large and sufficiently interested in your product or service to bring you as much business as you need/want? How did you determine the answer to this important question?

Exercise 10

Calculating Overhead Costs

For each of the following, estimate what your average monthly expense will be. For expenses that occur only once a year (license fees, magazine subscriptions and so on), divide by 12 to get the monthly expense. If you will have an expense that is partly attributable to the cost of operating your business and partly a personal expense (for example, your telephone bill), write in only that part that is business-related. If you don't expect to have a particular type of expense, leave the space blank. (See Chapter 3 for ideas on where to go for the information needed to complete this exercise.)

Business license, other permits   _____

Insurance premiums   _____

Telephone and utilities   _____

Maintenance of equipment, vehicles or workspace   _____

Stationery, office supplies   _____

Advertising   _____

Accounting, legal and other professional services   _____

Business-related dues, subscriptions and classes   _____

Other overhead expenses:

_____   _____

_____   _____

Total Overhead Costs Per Month   _____

How do you feel about this total? If it seems high, are there ways of cutting costs? How much business will be necessary to cover your monthly overhead costs?

Exercise 11

Deciding How Much to Charge

Your mini-business will perhaps involve several different products or services. If so, complete this exercise for the product or service you expect to provide most frequently.

1. If there is a product involved, what is its cost to you?

2. What is your average monthly overhead?   (Transfer your answer from Exercise 10.)

3. What is your initial guess as to a good price for your product or service?

4. How did you decide on this price? (Checked what others were charging and set my prices a little lower, asked potential customers what they'd be willing to pay, figured out how much I thought I should earn for my time, calculated the cost to me of my product and added on a percentage, etc.)

5. How many of the product will you have to sell in an average month (or how often will you have to provide the service) in order to cover your expenses?

(con't)

6. How many more will you have to provide in order to make the profit you
   need or want to make?

What do you conclude from this exercise? Is your proposed price realistic?
Do you think you'll be able to do as much business as necessary to meet your
financial goals? What would happen if you lowered your price? raised it?

Exercise 12

Choosing Ways to Spread the Word

For each of the following, make a check mark to indicate whether the method is appropriate to your type of business, whether you will be able to afford it in the beginning phases of your mini-business, and whether you think you would enjoy carrying it out. Are there any other criteria you should bring to bear in choosing ways to spread the word?

	Appropriate	*Affordable*	*Enjoyable*
Advertising			
Business cards............................	_____	_____	_____
Business stationery....................	_____	_____	_____
3x5 or 4x6 cards........................	_____	_____	_____
Flyers..	_____	_____	_____
Direct mail................................	_____	_____	_____
Referrals....................................	_____	_____	_____
Personal contact........................	_____	_____	_____
Portfolio....................................	_____	_____	_____
Newspaper classified ads..........	_____	_____	_____
Newspaper display ads..............	_____	_____	_____
Yellow pages.............................	_____	_____	_____
Signs...	_____	_____	_____
Customer gifts...........................	_____	_____	_____
Brochures..................................	_____	_____	_____
Local magazines........................	_____	_____	_____
Regional/national special interest magazines.................	_____	_____	_____
Trade shows..............................	_____	_____	_____
Directory listings......................	_____	_____	_____
Slide shows...............................	_____	_____	_____
Demonstrations.........................	_____	_____	_____
Free samples.............................	_____	_____	_____
Other:_____	_____	_____	_____

(con't)

Publicity

	Appropriate	Affordable	Enjoyable
Newspaper articles........................	_____	_____	_____
Television and/or radio...............	_____	_____	_____
Giving talks................................	_____	_____	_____
Teaching classes.........................	_____	_____	_____
Writing articles..........................	_____	_____	_____
Donations to community groups	_____	_____	_____
Participation in community affairs..................	_____	_____	_____
Other:_____	_____	_____	_____

What do you conclude from this exercise? Which method(s) will you use most extensively as you begin spreading the word of your mini-business? Which will you not use at all?

Exercise 13

Legal Requirements Checklist

Use this form to identify the laws and regulations that apply to your mini-business:

	Definitely applies	May apply	Does not apply	Where to learn more
Zoning and sign ordinances governing home businesses	____	____	____	City or county planning department
Business license	____	____	____	City or county clerk
Special permits	____	____	____	City or county clerk, county health department
Fictitious business name	____	____	____	County clerk
Other local requirements	____	____	____	City or county clerk
Seller's permit	____	____	____	State tax department
Occupational license	____	____	____	State department of consumer affairs
Articles of incorporation	____	____	____	State department of corporations
Other state requirements	____	____	____	State
Federal licenses and regulations	____	____	____	Federal Trade Commission
Insurance: liability	____	____	____	Insurance agent
multi-peril	____	____	____	Insurance agent
automobile	____	____	____	Insurance agent
other	____	____	____	Insurance agent

(con't)

	Definitely applies	May apply	Does not apply	Where to learn more
Federal identification number	____	____	____	I.R.S.
State identification number	____	____	____	State tax department
Regulations concerning businesses with employees (see Chapter 10)	____	____	____	I.R.S., state tax department, state department of industrial relations

Exercise 14

Skills and Knowledge I Need to Acquire

In this column, list skills and knowledge you need to acquire before beginning your mini-business.

Service or product offered

Advertising and publicity

Financial management

Other

In this column, write down how you will go about acquiring the needed skills or knowledge.

Exercise 15

Developing a Plan of Action

In the first column, make a list of the various tasks you need to accomplish in order to get your mini-business underway. Continue onto the back of the page if necessary. Then make check marks to indicate whether each task is absolutely essential (rather than of lesser importance) and timely (must be done sooner rather than later). Use this information to organize your tasks into a time line.

Tasks	*Essential*	*Timely*

Acknowledgements

Starting a Mini-Business is a revised and updated version of a booklet first published by New Ways to Work of Palo Alto, under a grant from the Luke B. Hancock Foundation. The exercises and other materials included in *Starting a Mini-Business* were developed together with Michael Closson who, in addition, read the initial version of the manuscript and made helpful suggestions for improving it. Thoughtful comments were also provided by Jane Benson and Mary Louise Tully. Dyanne Ladine, an attorney, and Bob Hunt, a certified public accountant, were consulted regarding the legal and financial information contained in these pages. The important work of copy editing and proof-reading was done by Kathleen Hallam, Steve Olsen, Susan Posnick, and Harry Wessenberg.

The wonderful illustrations are by Sara Boore who, along with Susan Cronin-Paris, is also responsible for the book design and graphics. It was a pleasure to work with two such gifted and congenial artists.

I am also grateful to Carol O'Hare of Fair Oaks Publishing for her enthusiastic confidence in the project and her talent for keeping things on track; to Betty Johnston who introduced me to a number of the mini-businesspeople profiled in these pages; and to all of the active seniors, pursuing retirement lives filled with usefulness and joy, who inspired the book and shared their stories with me.

About the Author

Nancy Olsen is not yet a senior, but in writing about mini-businesses, she speaks from experience. She has been Co-Director of New Ways to Work, where the ideas and materials in this book were first tested, and the proprietor of two small, at-home businesses. She now owns and operates a bookstore on Bainbridge Island, Washington.

How to Order Additional Books

Additional copies of *Starting a Mini-Business* may be ordered from the publisher. Send $8.95 plus $1.50 for shipping to Fair Oaks Publishing Company, 941 Populus Place, Sunnyvale, CA, 94086.

140

Index